SUFFOLK MISCELLANY

CLXX

SUFFOLK MISCELLANY

ALLAN JOBSON

CLXX

LONDON
ROBERT HALE & COMPANY

Composed by Specialised Offset Services Ltd, Liverpool
and printed in Great Britain by
Redwood Burn Limited, Trowbridge & Esher

CONTENTS

ILLUSTRATIONS

To
HUBERT ALLAN
A lover of Dunwich

FOREWORD

A miscellany is described as a book or magazine containing a number of compositions on miscellaneous subjects; a mixture of various kinds. That is surely what we understand by the word. However, in this case the subjects may be diverse, but there is a thread that connects them, from Agincourt to the Reform Bill, and that thread is Suffolk. When one comes to consider the link, it is surprising what the county has provided for our England. Yet, perhaps not surprising since the North Sea forms our eastern boundary, which contact made us what we are, an Anglo-Saxon race.

It may have been poor communications that led Mary Tudor to settle down among us, but one likes to think that she found it a pleasant country. Certainly the air was clean and the atmosphere free from intrigue. Her village home was stately as befitted a Tudor princess, and a refuge from the plague and the dreaded sweating sickness. I think she must have loved her garden with its little box borders, and perhaps she gathered the wild flowers with their intriguing names, such as penny pies, butter clocks, creeping Jenny, granny's bonnets, hedgehog holly and lambs' ears. We do know that she enjoyed the monks' garden at Butley, as also her visits to Eye. In the library of Queen's College, Oxford, is a finely illuminated book of hours, which belonged to her, and which she probably used at Bury and Westhorpe.

Then there was Cardinal Wolsey, a son of Ipswich and of Suffolk. It was said of him by a Bishop of London that he was the greatest political genius England ever produced. It is a curious fact that amongst his early appointments was that of Redgrave, on the presentation of the abbots of Bury. This was later to be the seat of the Bacon family. His dying lament came from his very soul. He described himself as a creation of the temperamental Henry, and like his master he could listen unmoved to the impassioned plea of Catherine of Aragon, which revealed the awful position of a royal lady in the days when the portals of the Tower of London were forever opening and closing on rich humanity.

It seems strange that Wolsey's downfall was speeded by a woman, one from Norfolk but who was so often in Suffolk – Anne Boleyn. Her beauty had caught the amorous eye of Henry. But she was to experience the vagaries of fortune when her time came. It was for long a tradition that her heart was laid up in a Suffolk church, a tradition that seemed to bear some foundation when a Victorian restoration was carried out at Erwarton Church and a heart-shaped leaden casket was found in the wall of the chancel. Anne was disliked by Mary Tudor, whose maid-of-honour she had been. It is her knot garden that still flourishes at Wolsey's Hampton Court.

Dunwich, the one-time capital city of East Anglia, has a history lost in time. It fascinated the Victorians, notably Edward FitzGerald. How he loved those old ruins, with that eccentric affection he could bestow on people and places. In his day the place was full of the Dix family; he used to stay with one and address his letters as from Dix Hall, renaming the spot Dixey Land. He seemed to draw his friends there, such as Charles Keene of *Punch*, whose mother was a Mary Sparrowe, or Sparowe, of the Ancient House, Ipswich. Then there was Edwin Edwards, painter and etcher, born at Halesworth. Old Fitz had a great regard for "the brave body but indifferent painter and his heroic wife". (He was always struggling against circumstances and his pictures did not sell).

FitzGerald took Carlyle there in 1855, and would have taken Lowell, if the latter's projected visit to him had materialised. And, I believe, Tennyson was made to walk its streets when he visited Fitz at Woodbridge. All these, with Swinburne, must have been impressed by the moving finger (of Time) that having writ moved on to write of a hamlet instead of a city.

Suffolk has had its nefarious episodes of witchcraft. There was Margery Jourdemayne, the celebrated witch of Eye who was consulted by the Duchess of Gloucester, wife of Duke Humphrey, and followed in the same place by Old Nan Barret. Margery finds a place in Shakespeare's *Henry VI*:

Bolingbroke	'What fates await the Duke of Suffolk?
Spirit	By water shall he die, and take his end.
Bolingbroke	'What shall befall the Duke of Somerset?'
Spirit	Let him shun castles:
	Safer shall he be upon the sandy plains
	Than where castles mounted stand.
	Have done, for more I hardly can endure.
Bolingbroke	Descend to darkness and the burning lake;
	False friend, avoid!

After the first battle of St Alban's, when the trembling monks crept out from their cells to succour the wounded and inter the slain, they found the dead body of Somerset lying at the threshold of a mean alehouse, the sign of which was a castle.

Suffolk provided its quota in the sordid witchcraft trials pursued with such ardour by Matthew Hopkins. This rascal charged twenty shillings for every town he visited, with a like sum for every convicted witch. He managed to dispose of forty at Bury alone, besides others scattered about such as at Lowestoft.

There were also the Suffolk martyrs, chronicled in Foxe's book. An early one was Thomas Bilney of Ipswich, "Little of stature and very slender of body". It was said that the greatness of his spirit made him a power among his contemporaries. He was brought to his death largely by the intervention of Wolsey.

And there was Will Dowsing, for whose birth Suffolk takes no credit. He destroyed much of pre-Reformation splendour in our churches, but he left that perfect piece of work, the Seven Sacrament Font at Cratfield. It is almost incredible to think that such perfection could be found tucked away in an obscure Suffolk village.

Suffolk has been always a superstitious county. Perhaps it was his early years and association that led Cardinal Wolsey to listen to some fortune tellers, as related by Fuller, that he should have his end at Kingston. His thoughts naturally turned to Kingston-on-Thames and it was said he would never ride through the town. It came home to him in the end when he realised it referred to Sir Anthony Kingston, Lieutentant of the Tower, who went to conduct him thither.

> The primrose to the grave is gone,
>   The Hawthorn flower is dead;
> The violet by a moss-grown stone
>   Has laid her weary head.

1

A Great Suffolk Lady

" 'Tis an old saying Like master, like man; why not as well, Like
Mistress, like maid."

In 1931 the Suffolk Institute of Archaeology and Natural
History published the *Household Book of Dame Alice de
Bryene*, for 1412-1413. She was the daughter of Robert de
Bures of Acton, a small village in West Suffolk, not far from
Long Melford. Her father died in April 1361, at the early age
of 27. Dame Alice married Sir Guy de Bryene of Oxenhalle,
Gloucester, who died February 1386 and was buried at
Slapton in Devon. His father, another Sir Guy, lived to be
ninety, and was buried at Tewkesbury.

Upon the death of her husband, the young widow returned
to her native village, making her abode at the manor house,
that she might be near her kinsfolk. Presumably her two
daughters came with her, Philippa and Elizabeth. After all,
that was her home and a brass of one of her ancestors was in
the church which she had attended in childhood, and
watched the shadows pass the east window as she turned the
pages of her missal. He was Sir Robert de Bures, died 1302
(modern scholarship makes this 1381), dressed in complete
chain mail, his crossed legs resting on a lion, his sword by his
side and his shield bearing his coat-of-arms.

Some of her kith and kin must have been at Agincourt on
that St Crispin's Day, fulfilling their only calling, that of
fighting, dressed in all the accoutrements of war. But she did
not remarry, remaining a widow for forty-four years, until
her own brass appeared, fifty-seven and a half inches high, in
widow's dress of veil, head-dress, barbe, kirtle and mantle,
her hands clasped in prayer, in the church where she had

prayed as a child. People make pilgrimage today to take rubbings of Sir Robert, because it is the finest brass in Suffolk and the finest military brass in all England, but they do not appear to be so interested in that of Dame Alice.

We might not have known much about the great lady if only her brass had survived, but it is her household book, written in contracted Latin, that has made her live and given us such a vivid picture of her life and times. To quote from the translators' introduction:

> Taken together, these accounts show the whole management of the household of a great Suffolk lady in the time of Agincourt. The day-book gives in detail the numbers who were fed at her table, and exactly what they ate down to the last pigeon or herring. It gives a picture of the loaves, white or black, baked by the hundred at frequent intervals, and sometimes on a Sunday; how they were stored in the pantry; and how many were issued for each day's consumption. It shows the amount of malt used on each brewing day and records how much of the ale was drunk daily, and how the wine was brought into store in the pantry and issued thence. It shows the small purchases made day by day for the kitchen, and how the horses of the household and of the guests were fed and bedded. It records the arrival of the fishmonger, and enters the date at which each cade of red herrings was begun. The lady not only took her meals with her household and her guests; she also demanded a strict account of all that they ate . . .

The purchases are of all kinds. They include payments for grain and cattle, fish, salt and spices; for the home manufacture of candles and tapers out of the kitchen fat; for repairs to buildings; for labourers employed in mowing the lady's meadows, and watchmen preventing the theft of her hay; or the shoeing of her horses; for kitchen utensils carefully recorded down to the earthen pans for catching dripping – the strainer priced 2d., the pestle also priced at 2d. – and for the sharpening of the kitchen knife.

The steward's stock-account covers also the poultry and game and herons, then a highly prized dish, the fish brought to the manor by a fish merchant or purchased at Stourbridge Fair (where the spices came from) by the lady; and the uses to which empty barrels were put. One old 'pipe' in which wine had arrived is turned into two washtubs for the laundress, another is converted into three 'keelers' for the bakehouse; other empties remain in store.

Among the lady's employees whose name appear, the more notable are John Fowler, shepherd; Robert Mose, smith; Richard Bonys, mower; John Colbrook, harvestman; John Skoyl, rent collector; and John White, farmer.

Here follows a summary of the victuals expended through-out an ordinary month (November): "Beef, one carcase, one pig, one young pig; one swan; 6 geese; mutton, II joints, 3 lambs; 4 capons; 4 chicken; 4 partridges; 147 pigeons (from the columbarium); 13 conies; 7 salt fish, 8 stock fish."

And this for a special month of January: "Beef, 2 carcases, one quarter; pork, 6 pigs; 3 chicken; 46 conies; 7 hens; red herrings 164; white herrings 400; 6 salt fish, 6 stock fish." One hundred oysters priced at 2d. were almost a daily occurence, but there is no mention of any venison and but few eels.

My mother was cradled in Suffolk in the 1850s of last century, the daughter of a farm labourer, in what was to all intents and purposes a mediaeval economy as practised by Dame Alice five hundred years before, even to the use of the same language. For example, the dish for catching the dripping when meat was roasting on the spit, was a latch pan, and this is what Moor had to say about it in his vocabulary: "Latch. To light or fall on any thing – a cat is said proverbially to 'allus latch on her legs'. The falling catch of a door or gate – 'Latch the door'. The pan into which the drippen or gravy of roasting meat falls or drips we call Latch pan."

Keelers were tubs used in brewing and washing. 'Keeler', or 'killer', was a Suffolk word for a shallow tub used for various purposes, such as a 'wash killer', 'milk killer', 'brewing killer'. Our keelers, writes Moor, "are sometimes raised on three feet, particularly those in dairies; but are not necessarily so."

Candles and rushlights were made in the farmhouse

kitchens from fat saved for the purpose, since there was little in the way of oil lamps until paraffin appeared about 1870. Candles played a great part when darkness fell, in fact they turned them into riddles:

> Little Miss Minafore
> Wears a white pinafore,
> The longer she sat
> The shorter she grew.

> Little Miss Mew
> Sat in a pew;
> The longer she sat
> The shorter she grew

In both cases the answer is a candle.

As there was no sanitation in the days of Dame Alice, so there was none in my mother's day. There was no alternative to the privy in the corner of the garden, overhung with ivy and the haunt of spiders and silver fish in its paper-lined walls. But it was a simple affair, and not a six-seater such as the one that has just been preserved by a government grant, the only one left in Britain, at Chilthorne Domer, near Yeovil, Somerset. The holes — for four adults and two children, all with lids — are set in a bench running round three walls.

Incidentally, Stourbridge or Sturbridge Fair was of very ancient foundation and was described as the largest in Europe. It was held in the river meadow a mile or two below Cambridge, from the middle of September until old Michael-mas, 11th October. It was evidently the prototype of Bunyan's "Vanity Fair".

Even in my mother's day the means of getting a light was by the tinder box, which is brought out by Lois Fison in one of her books published in 1899, quoting from the diary of an old Suffolk lady: "No box of matches was used in the old Suffolk days. On the high mantelpiece over the kitchen fireplace you would have seen the tinder box, in which was a flint and a bar of steel; at the bottom you would see the tinder-black burnt paper [rag]."

I don't think we should enjoy the food that the cook at Acton provided for the household, particularly the heron. There does not appear to have been a mill at Acton, so presumably the corn from the adjacent fields would have been ground at Long Melford, where the Abbot of Bury held sway, and was very jealous of his privileges.

The description of Acton as given by William White in his 1855 directory is not without interest. It opens with the fact that it was a pleasant village and that the old hall, now a farmhouse, was still moated. Acton Place was a seat of the Daniels family, who sold it in the early part of the eighteenth century to Robert Jennens Esq. He began the erection of an extensive and splendid mansion, which was finished by his son, William, who died in 1791 aged nearly a hundred, with the reputation of being the richest subject in the kingdom. On his death the fine tapestry was torn from the walls and sold. The mansion remained untenanted other than by an old man and woman, after which it was demolished except for the servants' wing; and the park and gardens became cultivated fields.

2

The White Queen

A shielded scutcheon blush'd with blood of queens and kings.

Keats

Some twenty miles north of Acton is a tiny village, almost too small to be marked on the average map. Its name is Westhorpe, and when White compiled his directory it consisted of only 240 souls. In the delightful little church, now rather neglected and in decay, is a modern tablet which records the fact that Mary Tudor, third daughter of Henry VII King of England, formerly lived in this parish and that she was Queen of France.

The birth of Mary Tudor, although of rather uncertain date, has been placed in 1495. Attempts have been made to denigrate her beauty, but as so many portraits of her exist and they all convey a similar likeness, contemporary accounts are not all exaggerations. She was supposed to have been like her mother, Elizabeth of York, with fair hair and blue eyes. Erasmus described her as "Divinely pretty, soft, pleasant, gentle and charming as the Muses". And again, writing to a friend when she was bethrothed to Prince Charles of Castile: "Nature never formed anything more beautiful and she excels no less in goodness and wisdom." Certainly her oval face looks out today, as painted by an unknown artist, clear and lovely. She was undoubtedly a desirable person and wealthy withal, and when she got to France this was said of her: "A distinguished person . . . blonde, without being colourless, of slightly accented features, but regular, with an air of grandeur and much elegance; of a distinctly English rose-coloured beauty." Moreover, she was quick-witted, independent and as obstinate as any of her family.

21

Her marriage to Charles took place by proxy at Greenwich, on 13th August 1514, but was never fulfilled. Unfortunately, like other eligible princesses, she was married off, in her case to the middle-aged French King, Louis XII, at Abbeville (so well-known a town in World War I), in the same year as her proxy marriage to Charles. This Tudor Rose must have looked remarkably fair, in cloth of gold on crimson trimmed with ermine, when Louis clasped a jewel round her neck. He had previously bestowed on her a magnificent gift, known as the 'Mirror of Naples', which was a jewelled diamond as large as a man's finger, with a pear-shaped pearl beneath, the size of a pigeon's egg. This was said to be worth 60,000 crowns and caused a lot of controversy when Louis died. He also gave her fortysix diamond and ruby ornaments. Mrs Everett Green says that when Mary went to France her suite included six maids of honour, two chamber maids, four lords, six bannerettes; seventeen knights and eight esquires; besides fifty officers of her household, her usher, serjeant-at-arms, almoner, secretary, physician and two chaplains. The French king complained of this multitude, so the suite was reduced to an almoner, chaplain, master of the horse, physician, three pages of honour, master of the pantry, cup-bearer, carver, usher groom of the robes, and six ladies. But she must have eclipsed the lot because the Venetain ambassador declared: "She is a Paradise."

It is interesting to note that Louis XII was the son of Charles d'Orleans, who had spent a quarter of a century as a prisoner in England, having been taken at Agincourt. Louis has been described as infirm, diseased and stricken with gout, though his conduct to his new bride suggests he was a man she could respect. However, the marriage lasted but eighty-four days, the King dying on New Year's Day, 1515, the same age as Mary's father, fifty-two. This was hardly of old age in our sense of the word. Unfortunately for poor Mary, she was now alone in France, because when he complained of the size of her entourage, Louis had dismissed her bosom companion, Lady Guildford because he said she interfered between himself and the Queen.

As it was uncertain as to whether Mary was pregnant, and if with a son, which would have altered the succession to the French throne, she was forced to remain in seclusion at the Hotel de Cluny in Paris for six weeks; and as she was always dressed in white she became known as the White Queen. It was then that she got embarassed by Francis of Valois, who was heir presumptive. His courtly approaches to her became rather warmer than was necessary, or than his wife could endure. According to hearsay, she had told her brother, who had instigated the marriage to Louis, that she had allowed herself to be used for reasons of state once, but the next time it would be to please herself.

Charles Brandon, Duke of Suffolk, who had been brought up as a boy with Henry VIII, and had been on ambassadorial work in France, was sent over to escort Mary home and to be sure to bring her dowry with her and any marriage presents she had received. These were numerous, including the Mirror of Naples, which the wife of the now Francis I of France, declared was hereditary property of the Queens of France. In fact Brandon married Mary, at the great risk of gaining the wrath of the King. They were married at the Cluny chapel in Paris by an unknown priest. It is certain that Mary was greatly in love with him. (He was of Brandon, Suffolk, and had relationship with the Wingfield family of Letheringham.)

Henry VIII had created Charles Brandon Duke of Suffolk in 1514. His father, a country squire, had joined Henry VII in 1485 and became his standard bearer. He was killed by Richard III's own hand at Bosworth. Henry VII then adopted him and he was brought up with the royal children and thus became a close friend of the future Henry VIII.

In Henry VII's time he married Anne, daughter of Sir Anthony Browne; this was annulled on grounds of consanguinity and he then proceeded to marry a rich widow, Margaret Mortimer. Tiring of her he re-married Anne Browne, by whom he had two daughters. She died in 1512. He then proceeded to marry Elizabeth Grey, but this marriage was annulled. Although then legally single, he had two ex-wives when he married Mary Tudor.

At first Henry was in a great rage when he heard of his sister's new alliance, but he was soon pacified by the amount of the dowry returned and by a large sum of money levied on Brandon. The uncertainty of the authenticity of that Paris wedding was regulated by another, celebrated at Greenwich on Sunday 13th May 1515. She then became known as the Queen Duchess. Henry, their eldest child, was born on 17th July 1516. Two girls were also born to them, Frances and Eleanor. Their first home was Suffolk Place at Southwark.

When Mary attended that fantastical pageant known as the 'Field of the Cloth of Gold,' she was said to have led a procession of lords and ladies to the French camp, "scintillating in her saddle". She and her husband were accompanied by five chaplains, twenty-four ladies and gentlemen, fifty-five servants, and thirty horses with grooms. Henry and Wolsey crossed over with a suite of some five thousand, while some six thousand workmen had been sent over to make the necessary preparations.

Although Mary's life was set in splendour in that fascinating Tudor period, it would almost appear that of all the residences open to her she preferred Westhorpe, where she set about re-modelling the gardens in the French manner. If nothing else it provided a refuge from the plague, which so often attacked the large towns. In any case it was no mean dwelling and according to an assessment for 1526, she had amongst her establishment forty-three men and seven women, including two knights, one esquire and a Frenchman. And this is what White said about it in his 1855 directory:

It was the manor of William de la Pole, Duke of Suffolk when he was beheaded in 1450. It was afterwards granted to Chas Brandon, Duke of Suffolk, who married as his third wife Mary Tudor, Dowager Queen of France and sister to Henry VIII, and here they resided in great splendour at Westhorpe Hall, which was demolished many years ago. The cloisters, the chapel, with its painted windows, and the original furniture were kept up until about 90 years ago, when the whole was taken down, and a farmhouse was built on its site, which is still moated. Martin, who witnessed the demolition, said it was done in a careless manner, all the fine chimneys and ornaments being pulled down with ropes and crushed to pieces.

Just as Dame Alice relied on Stourbridge Fair for her spices etc, so Mary and Charles attended the famous Bury Fair, originally granted to the monastery in 1135 by Henry I and held for six days, around the feast of St James. "During the celebrations of the great fair of Bury, a splendid tent or pavilion was erected in the great court of the abbey, for the accommodation of Mary Queen of France; in which she received the compliments of the nobility and gentry, who resorted to Bury to join in the amusements and entertainments that the town, at that time of the fair, peculiarly afforded."

Although Mary had been used to the pomp and circumstance of Tudor court life, yet it is quite evident that she loved her Suffolk retreat. This is shown by her visits to Butley Abbey in the time of Augustine Rivers. Staverton Forest, the wild country between Melton and Hollesley, and the salt marshes of the sea, provided excellent sport; and the Dukes of Norfolk and Suffolk, together with Lord Willoughby, who all owned property at Bawdsey, bordering on those of the priory, were frequently entertained there.

Mary was often there and her first recorded stay was in 1515-16 when she dates a letter to Wolsey on 28th September. She was apparently there again in the autumn of 1518, when her husband dated a letter to Wolsey from Butley on 23rd September. A year later she wrote herself to Wolsey from Butley on 28th September 1519, and in 1527 she is said to have stayed in the priory for two months with her husband. On the 6th August, as it was very hot," she ordered her supper to be laid out in a shady part of the garden at the eastern side of the house". This was very successful, and she had picnic suppers on several occasions in one or the other of the little gardens belonging to the brethren. On 21st August, however, while in Brother Nicholas's garden, the royal party was overtaken by a storm and hastily retreated into the church. Mary seems to have been fond of these alfresco meals, because on June 1528, we are told, that she and her husband rode to Staverton for a fox-hunt and dined there under the oaks.

Mary Tudor died at Westhorpe in June 1533, of a decline that was to be the common lot of women until almost our own time. She had not been satisfied with the treatment she had received from her own doctor and had expressed a wish that she might have gone to London to be under her brother's doctor. But the journey was too great. It might even have been in her mind that Henry himself could have done something for her, because amongst his other accomplishments he dabbled in medicine, and kept a record of all sorts of ointments and pills. He even volunteered advice on such matters.

She was buried with much pomp in the Abbey Church at Bury. Her body lay in state under a blue velvet pall in the chapel at Westhorpe Hall for three weeks. It is said the long funeral procession, headed by the Lady Frances walking between her husband and her brother, left the Hall on the Monday and reached Bury at 2 p.m. the next day; a distance of fourteen miles. What a cavalcade there must have been, with candles burning and priests chanting. An account of her funeral is in the College of Arms, together with a list of the mourners. In the manuscript it is stated that the "officers of the chauntry and the clerks of the spicery came and cered the queen with linen cloth, wax and with a number of spices very costly".

The funeral car which was hung with banners displaying the insignia of the Tudors — a dun cow, a hawthorn bush and a portcullis — was drawn by six chargers draped in black velvet embroidered with the Tudor rose and the lilies of France. A golden pall had replaced the blue velvet. It must have been a long cavalcade, with the chief mourners added to by a hundred pensioners in black gowns and hoods carrying tapers; a concourse of knights, barons, clergy; followed by Clarencieux and Norry King-at-Arms.

Then came ten of Mary's ladies, each attended by a groom, with maidservants and others bringing up the rear.

The coffin was received by the Bishop of Lincoln and the abbot and monks of Bury. The church, hung with heraldic banners bearing French and English escutcheons, was completely filled, so that the tenantry had to stand outside.

The next morning two low masses were said, followed by a requiem mass in the afternoon, and an address was given by the abbot of St Benet's Abbey. When the leaden coffin was about to be lowered into the vaults, it appears that a disturbance was caused by the sudden irruption of Mary's two step-daughters, the Ladies Powis and Monteagle, with their husbands, who insisted in taking the lead. Requiem masses were also said at Westminster Abbey and St Paul's Cathedral.

Mary's kindnesses were not forgotten, neither was the great dole, which was distributed after the first funeral dinner. There were four points in Bury at which meat and drink was available to all, and every poor person received four pennies.

Unfortunately, her remains were not allowed to rest in peace. When the dissolution of the abbey took place, her coffin was removed to St Mary's Church and buried under a slab of Petworth marble, marked at each corner and in the centre with a cross, so it had evidently been consecrated. It may have been an altar slab removed from the abbey church under the reforming hand of Edward VI.

In 1731 the tomb was again disturbed. On this occasion the casket was opened by the curious, to find that the embalming had been effective and that her hair had retained its colour and was of considerable length. Also her teeth were in excellent condition. Not satisifed with gazing on a former beauty, some cut off locks of her hair, and in 1786 one was put up for sale, when it fetched £6 10s. Another lock was sold in 1848 for £7 10s. Horace Walpole is said to have bought a locket of the hair for 52s. 6d. Some doubt surrounds some of these sales as there was said to have been a woman in Bury with similar hair who may have been persuaded to part with some of her own for the purpose. A lock is to be seen in Moyse's Hall.

Edward VII in 1904 authorised the altar slab covering the grave in the north-east corner of the chancel to be enclosed by a marble curb. Queen Victoria presented the easternmost window in the south aisle in Mary's memory. This depicts the marriage of Mary Tudor with Louis XII of France, at Abbeville, the nuptials being solemnised by Cardinal de Brie and two bishops; a canopy of gold is borne by the Dukes of Angoulême and Alencon. Mary is also represented making her entry into Paris, with Francis of Valois (afterwards Francis I) riding on her side. Then comes Mary, '*Le Reine Blanche*', in her widowhood, seated in her apartment of the Hotel de Cluny, lit only by wax tapers. Charles Brandon is conversing with her.

In the lower portion of these lights are depicted the visit of Erasmus and Sir Thomas More to the young children of Henry VII at Eltham; the betrothal to the Prince of Castile in the King's Presence Chamber at Richmond. The Archbishop of Canterbury is the chief officiating prelate, and Mary is seen kneeling beside the Lord de Bergues, who acted as proxy for the Prince of Castile. Then comes the embarcation of Mary at Dover on her voyage to France. At the foot of the steps near which she is standing, taking leave of Queen Catherine of Aragon, there is a glimpse of the sea and of one of the vessels of the royal fleet; Henry VIII is also close at hand as Mary quits the English shore. (It might be mentioned that Mary was very fond of Catherine and was against the idea of divorce.)

The three lower compartments represent the marriage to Charles Brandon in the oratory chapel of the Hotel de Cluny in the presence of Francis I, the reception of Mary by Henry VIII on her return to England and the interment of her remains in the abbey church at St Edmundsbury. In the traceries above are portraits of Mary Tudor, Henry VIII, the

Prince of Castile, Louis XII and the Duke of Suffolk, with their armorial bearings beneath them. The smaller openings are filled with the Tudor rose and other ornaments. Here then are shown in glass the principle events in the life of the quondam Queen of France.

It would appear that Victoria had somewhat of an affinity with Mary in her own marriage to the Prince Consort. Because, not since Mary married the Duke of Suffolk had a princess married with the sovereign's official sanction outside the confines of a reigning house. Also, until Victoria and the Prince Consort visited the French royal family at the Chateau d' Eau in 1843, no visit had been paid by the English royal family since the days of Henry VIII.

Although Brandon had contracted so many marriages, he was soon to seek another. This time he chose Catherine Lady Willoughby, of Eresby, by whom he had two sons, both of whom died without issue. He survived Mary by about ten years, dying of the dreaded sweating sickness. His son by Mary also died young, therefore his line died out.

Mary's elder daughter, Frances, married Henry Grey, Marquis of Dorset. It was her daughter, Lady Jane, "who suffered for the rashness of her friends"; and it was her sister, Catherine, who died in captivity in Yoxford, probably inheriting the beauty of her grandmother as also her disease. Her crime was that of her grandmother, marrying the Earl of Hertford for love, without permission.

3

Framlingham Castle and Mary I, 1518-58

When I am dead and opened, you shall find 'Calais' lying in my heart. Holinshed.

It is surprising how much of the English story lies within those old walls of a Suffolk castle, situate in a Suffolk market town. As old John Wodderspoon reminds us: "The Castle of Framlingham, whether considered as a relic of antiquity – the hold of feudality – or a building with which some of the most celebrated historical acts are connected, has strong claims upon the attention."

Here the Bigods reigned, the Mowbrays, Howards and Brothertons; and in the nearby church lies the body of Henry Fitzroy, Duke of Richmond and natural son of Henry VIII. Some of these were very near the throne yet never gained it. From here also issued forth Bloody Mary to gain her crown; and it is with her that we are chiefly concerned.

It seems rather strange to read of Mary Tudor (otherwise known as Bloody Mary to distinguish her from her aunt, the White Queen of France), that she was by nature kind and considerate, showing those qualities in her private life in her treatment of her servants, her ladies and the poor folk that lived about her.

The early years of her life had been gloomy and stormy enough. Her father had alternatively threatened to make her a nun and have her beheaded; and he and his ministers had forced her to sign a paper in which she formally acknowledged that the church she adored was a cheat, and that the mother who bore her had never been her father's lawful wife.

However, following the attachment to music inherited in the Tudor family, when her mother was finally separated

31

from Henry, Catherine wrote to her exhorting her to suffer cheerfully, to trust in God, and keep her heart clean, adding "and sometimes for recreation use your virginals and lute, if you have any".

Her early portrait shows a very resolute little woman, heavily bejewelled, tight lipped and with clenched hands. She was undoubtedly fond of her father in spite of his uncertain temperament, and from all accounts he returned her affection. But she was also staunch to her mother. When the divorce became established and Anne Boleyn was proclaimed queen, Mary exclaimed, "I know no Queen in England but my mother. But if you, Madam, as my father's mistress, will intercede for me with him, I should be grateful."

Again, when Elizabeth was born and Mary was desired to pay her respects to the baby princess, she replied that she knew no Princess of England but herself, and burst into tears.

Anne Boleyn's treatment of this small step-daughter showed how she feared her, whose only crime was loyalty to her abandoned mother. It also becomes apparent when reading modern biographies that if ever Anne should have acted as regent, she would have had both mother and daughter executed. It was surely a curious twist of fortune that when Anne was despatched, both these little princesses were delcared illegitimate. However, although Mary and all her supporters were delighted at the fall and execution of Anne (the usurper as she was thought of by many), Mary prayed for her soul.

When one considers Mary's steadfastness as a child — to her religion and her mother — and the cruelty of the times, it may account for her fierceness in later years. Because her cruelty to her Protestant subjects as she grew older became almost phenomenal. If Henry VIII was good with the axe, her use of the burning faggot was almost beyond belief. It is recorded that Henry VII burned ten heretics in twenty-four years; Henry VIII eightyone in thirty-eight years; Elizabeth five in forty-four years. But Mary attained a grand total of 283 in five years. These were, of course, apart from political executions.

John Fox, the martyrologist (1554-8), wrote:

> What eyes thou readest with, reader, know I not,
> Mine were not dry when I her story wrote.

True, many of these martyrdoms were the result of the machinations of dark-hearted men, like Stephen Gardiner, but there were others, such as Cardinal Pole. And if she had but listened to the voice of Simon Renard, a diplomat from the Court of Charles V, Elizabeth her successor would have been put out of the way, to ensure a continuance of the papal dominance. As it was the young Elizabeth spent some months in the Tower, and had to crave pardon for the error of her ways on her knees before her sister.

When Edward VI came to the throne, he held his first court at Framlingham, the castle having fallen into his hands through its seizure by his father. At the end of his short reign it passed into the possession of Mary. It was uncertain for a brief while as to who would succeed, as her supporters proclaimed the unfortunate Lady Jane Grey, who —

> Was so good a lady
> That no tongue dare yet
> Prounance dishonour of her.

And Mary's Romish character rendered her rather uncertain. Robert Rochester, comptroller of her household, arranged for her to escape from her Essex home where she was staying, through Malden. But Mary wisely demurred, because she rightly decided that if she left England she would never be queen. Instead, she made her way to Kenninghall in Norfolk when the Norfolk and Suffolk gentry came and offered to fight for her. The gentlemen and people of Buckinghamshire and Oxford also rose on her behalf. She was therefore proclaimed queen at Kenninghall, upon which she moved to Framlingham Castle. This was easier to defend than Kenninghall and was nearer to the sea if she found it necessary to escape to Flanders.

The Earl of Northumberland, supporting Lady Jane Grey, had sent a fleet to Yarmouth to prevent Mary's escape. On 13th July 1553 this mutined and declared for her. The Earl also heard that she had been joined by almost all the inhabitants of Suffolk and the adjoining counties. These amounting to some thirteen thousand men encamped near the castle. Northumberland heard it was forty thousand. She was certainly welcomed to the throne when she reached London.

It was surely a curious turn of events, that when she was younger the Duke of Norfolk intrigued to marry his eldest son, the poet Surrey, to her as Princess Mary, thus enabling him to claim the throne. And it is in Framlingham church that Surrey's beheaded body lies, near the tomb of his father who escaped Henry's axe by only a day.

Mary's character on the throne was soon established. Ridley, who was to be one of her martyrs, offered to preach to her. Her reply was that she had never read a Protestant book. "My Lord for your gentlemen to come and see me, I thank you; but for your offering to preach before me, I thank you never a whit."

As far as Suffolk, was concerned, her most important victim was Rowland Taylor, parson of Hadleigh, of whom J.R. Green the historian writes so highly, of his courage and joyful character. He was one of the first martyrs of the reign, chosen by Gardiner. Quoting Green, his wife, "suspecting that her husband should that night be carried away, had waited through the darkness with her children in the porch of St Botolph's beside Aldgate. Now when the sheriff his company came against St. Botolph's Church, Elizabeth cried, saying, 'O my dear father! Mother! mother! here is my father led away!' Then cried his wife, 'Rowland, Rowland, where art thou?' — for it was a very dark morning, that the one could not see the other. Dr Taylor answered, 'I am here, dear wife,' and stayed. The sheriff's men would have led him forth, but the sheriff said, 'Stay a little, masters, I pray you, and let him speak to his wife.' "

He was then taken back to Hadleigh, and when he was paying the price with the greatest courage on Aldham Common, one of his executioners "cruelly cast a faggot at him, which hit him upon his head and brake his face that the blood ran down his visage. Then said Dr Taylor, 'O friend, I have harm enough — what needed that?'"

When Mary grew old and near her end, this is how Michele the Venetian ambassador described her:

> She is a woman of low stature, but has no defects in her limbs, nor any deformity whatever. In person she is thin and delicate; altogether unlike her father, who was tall and big; and her mother, who, if tall, was stout, the face is well formed; and according to the portraits of her which were seen when she was younger, she was not only good looking, but more than middling pretty. At present, besides some wrinkles caused more by sorrow than by age, which make her appear older than she is, her face is very grave. Her eyes are so piercing as to induce not only reverence, but fear, in those she turns them on; and yet she is very short-sighted-being unable to read, or do anything else, without placing her eyes quite close to the object. Her voice is thick and loud, like a man's; so that when she speaks she is always heard a good way off. In short, she is a decent woman of her age; and putting aside her rank as queen, she would never be abhorred for ugliness.

In 1554, Mary married Philip of Spain, who disappeared in spite of her passionate entreaties to stay, when all hope of a child was abandoned. It is interesting to recall the value set upon clothes and especially jewelry by the Tudors; when Mary died, Sir Nicholas Throckmorton was admitted to see the corpse, and as Elizabeth had requested, took from her finger the wedding ring which had been given by Philip and delivered it to Elizabeth.

In 1580 the religious wheel of doctrine turned full circle and Framlingham Castle became a prison for recusants. Two important Acts of Parliament were passed in Elizabeth's reign. One in 1558 restored to the Crown "the ancient Jurisdiction over the State Ecclesiastical and Spiritual, and abolishing all Foreign Power repugnant to the same".

The second was an Act passed the same year "for the

Uniformity of Common Prayer and Divine Service in the Church and the Administration of the Sacrament".

The choice of Framlingham was made by Sir Francis Walsingham, one of the Secretaries of State. Amongst the commissioners who exercised a general supervision over the prison were such gentlemen as Sir Robert Jermyn, of Rushbrooke Hall, Sir John Higham and Robert Ashfield, Esquire. A man named Thomas Pooley was appointed by the Council as keeper.

When the original commissioners vacated office, their places were taken by Sir Arthur Heveningham, of Heveningham; Sir Nicholas Bacon, of Redgrave, who had been Sheriff of Norfolk and Suffolk, and was half brother of the Francis Bacon who became Lord Chancellor; Sir Anthony Wingfield, of Letheringham, who had been Sheriff of Suffolk; Henry Gawdy, of Redenhall, a former Sheriff of Norfolk; Thomas Rouse, Esq., and Robert Barker Esq. There were thirty-six prisoners. Thus a sovereign's palace became a prison and so continued until March 1603.

> Still stand thy battlemented towers,
> Firm as in bygone years;
> As if, within, yet ruled the powers
> Of England's haughtiest peers.
>
> Bernard Barton

4

Tudor Suffolk

This blessed plot, this earth, this realm, this England.

It is rather interesting to speculate as to what the Suffolk countryside was like in those days of the Tudors. Enclosure were not yet and the yeoman prevailed below the manorial lords. It must have been well wooded, especially in High Suffolk. Even the coastline had its share of timber, because the old records give an Eastwood and a Westwood for Dunwich, although that old capital of East Anglia was struggling for existence against the all powerful sea, and more than half of it had gone.

A very interesting list of farm implements and livestock which had to be maintained on the manor of the time of Edward I on the decease of each bishop, has been preserved which presumably held good in Tudor times. They are as follows:

There should remain in stock ten steers for two ploughs, [the plough team would have consisted of oxen with their wide wooden yokes], for waggon one cart horse of the value of 13/4, twelve cows at the price of half a mark, one bull, three sows, one boar, twenty-six ewes and twenty-seven and one wethers.

Two brazen pots, one brass pan, one cauldron, two tripods, two furnaces or ovens, six great cildelades, three great tuns, two small, three troughs, one napkin, one towel, seed, ironwork, tools, one servant, one prepositus [foreman], two bercarii [shepherds], one cowherd to be provided and maintained out of the estate of the deceased until the festival of the chains of St Peter [Lammas Day, 1st August], and there should remain also one iron-bound cart and others not iron bound, with all the harness.

From the beginning of his reign Henry VII had devoted himself to objects of peace, to the removal of scars which the Wars of the Roses had left. However, all was not well because as early as 1086 Domesday recorded that in Suffolk alone five thousand acres of arable land were being held by religious houses, and during the period of the Crusades and the great religious activity of the twelfth and thirteenth centuries the Church, by gift and purchase, had increased the holding tenfold. Thrail said the great fear was that ultimately all England might become church property. Moreover there were still bondmen in England in the sense of being tied to the soil.

Then came the complaint: "Halfe England ys nowght now but shepe." "A land glad with corn-fields no longer rejoiced the farmer's heart. Every year less and less land came under the plough, and wool was at once the riches and the curse of the country."

J.R. Green in his history says:

The steady rise in the price of wool was at this period giving a fresh impulse to the agriarian changes which had been going steadily on for the last hundred years, to the throwing together of the smaller holdings, and the introduction of sheep-farming on an enormous scale. The merchant classes, too, were investing largely in land, and these "farming gentlemen and clerking knights," as Latimer (1488-1555), bitterly styled them, were restrained by few traditions or associations in their eviction of the smaller tenants ... "My father," says Latimer, "was a yeoman and had no lands of his own; only he had a farm of three or four pounds by the year at the uttermost, and hereupon he tilled so much as kept half a dozen men. He had a walk for a hundred sheep, and my mother milked thirty kine; he was able and did find the King's harness with himself and his horse while he came to the place that he should receive the King's wages. I can remember that I buckled his harness when he went to Blackheath Field. He kept me to school: he married my sisters with five pounds apiece, so that he brought them up in godliness and fear of God. He kept hospitality for his poor neighbours and some alms he gave to the poor, and all this he did of the same farm, where he that now hath it payeth sixteen pounds by year or more, and is not able to do anything for his prince, for himself, nor for his children, or give a cup of drink to the poor." The bitterness of ejection was increased by the inquitous means which were often employed to bring it about. The farmers, if we believe More, were "got rid of either by fraud or force, or tired out with repeated wrongs into parting with their property." "In this way it comes to pass that these poor wretches, men, women, husbands, orphans, widows, parents with little children, households greater in number than in wealth (for arable farming requires many hands, while one shepherd and herdsman will suffice for a pasture farm), all these emigrate from their native fields without knowing where to go." The sale of their scanty household stuff drove them to wander homeless abroad, to be thrown into prison as vagabonds, to beg and to steal. Yet in face of such a spectacle as this we still find the old complaint of the scarcity of labour, and the old legal remedy for it in a fixed scale of wages.

One wonders how Alice de Bryene got about, or Mary Tudor for that matter. Of the latter we are told that the roads were so bad and the journeys so fatiguing that she was glad to stay at Westhorpe. In fact the journey to and from London via Ipswich helped to bring about her end. Presumably even the journey to and from Butley Abbey would have been made more easily by the old Roman roads. These were to remain to our own days and still do even with the advent of the motor roads. The Reverend Alfred Suckling writing in 1846, and that was not all that removed from Tudor Suffolk in character and economy, says that in 1839 there were 281 miles of turnpike roads and 3,235 of other highways. Those other leave a wide question mark, with the era of the stone breaker, his goggles and his hammer. The ruts and puddles must have been appalling and a hazard to life.

But dear old Reyce goes one better and has this to say:

I must confess as all other earthly benefits are accompanied with some incommodities, it is objected it (the county) lyeth open, and is ready for foreign invasion, there bee so many havens, harbours, creeks, and other places of ready discent, that the enemy is soon entered ... Butt that which is common to all other sea-bordering shires (as what shore is free from their insulting, audacious, and

their furtive preying) ought nott here to be reckoned as a
particular incommoditie, neither may their furtive assaults with a
more momentary returne bee reputed as a warlike invasion, which
whensoever it shall bee effected, by that time the invaders meet
with our deep myrie soyle, our narrow and fowle lanes, our
manifold inclosures, severed with so many deep ditches, hedges,
and store of wood, bushes and trees, seeing the impassableness of
this Country, with any martiall forces, albeit there were noe other
meanes of resistance, they will have just cause to repent their
rashnesse.

From the foregoing one can hardly have a clearer picture
of the state of things. However, it must be recorded that
the air was pure. It was Keats who remarked that the air of
Hampshire was worth sixpence a pint.

Our numerous rivers abounded with fish such as "trout,
barbel and Crevices", together with chub, pike, and eels so
much relished, especially when stuffed. There was even a
pikemonger among the various tradesmen. And not for-
getting our local speciality, the herring, which Dame Alice
made good use in providing for her numerous visitors. Even
an occasional sturgeon, because one was caught as late as
1753 above Beccles bridge, weighing eleven stone two
pounds.

Bird life was abundant, with many predators such as
eagle, osprey, gyrfalcon, kestrel, merlin, buzzard, sparrow-
hawk and eagle owl. Then follows the long-eared, short-
eared and tawny owls; great shrike, red-backed and wood-
chat shrike; spotted and pied flycatcher; water and ring
ouzel; and golden oriel.

Then come wheatear, grasshopper — reed and wood
warbler; bearded titmouse, waxen chatterer, snow bunting;
bramble and haw finches; tree sparrow, siskin; lessr and
mealy redpole; mountain linnet or twite, crossbill, rose-
coloured ouzel, raven and bee-eater; great, little and thick-
necked bustard; bittern, night heron, white stork, spotted
redshank, greenshank, avocet, great snipe, purple sandpiper;
bean, white-fronted, bernicle and brent geese, various

ducks, including red-breasted merganser and goosander; various grebe including great northern and red-throated diver; foolish guillemot, little auk, puffin and razorbill, gannet, a number of tern and gulls, ending up with the stormy petrel.

In the Household Book of Hengrave for January 1573 is the entry: "To Gyle of Bury for VII mallards, V curlews, VI teales, iiij knottes, j plover, and XXX stints, bought together XIXs. iijd."

There is a long list of wild flowers and grasses, with the most interesting collection of names. One wonders who gave them such descriptive labels, and if either Mary Tudor or Dame Alice collected them as they took their walks. There were, for instance, suffocated, rough and flat-headed clovers; stinking goose-foot, spotted cat's-ear, treacle mustard, sneezewort, mudwort, and whorled water milfoil; smooth finger, bulbous meadow and cord were all grasses; together with two-staminal, pendulous, beaked and bottle sedge. The worts consisted of squinancy, saltwort, mother-wort, figwort, march fleawort and sea pearlwort; together with shepherd's cress, field penny cress and creeping yellow cress. Now followed bastard toadflax, sowbane, red goose-foot, spanish catchfly, branched broomrape, dusky cranesbill, man and bog orchids, early spider orchid, breck-land wormwood. There were also sea heather, sea holly and sea spurge. One is also pleased to remember there were wild tulips, snake's-head frittilary, purple crocus, spiked speed-well, pale flax, cyclamen, marsh mallow and the hairy violet.

The list also includes meadow saffron, water plantain, yellow vetch, yellow or sickle medick, greater or rough hawk's-beard, summer snowflake and alkanet. Now follow umbellate chickweed, chaff weed, hairy greenweed, red-veined dock, narrow-leaved redmace, chervil, corinder, cut-leaved dead-nettle, perennial knawel, large wintergreen, spring cinquifoil and yellow star thistle.

But I must also mention the very scarce crested buckler-fern which was only found at Westleton, and the daphne mezereum, of which an old doctor's herbal in my possession states: "It is said to grow about Laxfield in Suffolk ... the bark and berries in different forms, have been long externally used to obstinate ulcers and ill-conditioned sores ... In this country it is employed for the cure of some syphilitic complaints."

In the old days there was but one High Sheriff for the two counties and this continued until 1576, when Robert Ashfield, of Stowlangtoft, Esq., held that high office, while Sir Arthur Hopton was the first Knight of the Shire in Parliament for the county. And there were fairs in great numbers, Suckling lists seventy-two.

Another rather interesting fact was that women exceeded men in number, and that "Suffolk fair maids" was no uncertain commendation, brought about, it was thought, by the great number of cows which grazed in those flower-strewn meadows and the consequent large supply of milk.

In this connection Gage in his *Antiquities of Hengrave* quotes from a Household Book of Thomas Kytson for 1572

a somewhat unique custom of presenting a purse to members of his household at Hengrave on the occasion of their marriage:

"In reward to Stephen, Mr Longe's man, at my master his commandment, viz to a purse made for him at his marriage vjs" with this footnote:

The copies of a letter to the tenants: "Whereas a cople of Mr Kytson's servants are, by God's grace, to be married about Mich. next; even which time I am in some doubt of his return beyond the seas, and therefore wold be loth to trouble his good neighbours and friends in the countries hereabouts, with desire of these travell and charges at the same; yet being desirous of their preferment and well doing, and thinking, in the time of my husband's absence that I may be more bold with the inhabitants within his owne townes, and tenants of his manors, belonging to the same, than elsewhere; this shall be earnestly to desire you not only, against that time, to contribute such provision of money, as, and my request, at this time, and for both our sakes, you can like to bestow on them, to a purse which I herewith send you by this bearer, but also, in your means, to require every such inhabitant, and well willing tenant, belonging to the same, as you can think mete, to do the lyke. In accomplishment whereof, as I will think myself beholding to you and them, so I am sure, at his return he will therefore be right thankful to every one of you, and the rather for your good will shewed in this behalf in the time of his absence. And so with my further commemdacions I bid you farewell."

Here follows an extract from a manuscript in Domestic State Papers of certain notable Suffolk men of the time of Queen Elizabeth, dated 18th January 1593. This was contributed by Walter Rye, who states the text is by Maynard, Lord Burghley's clerk, alterations and corrections by Cecil: "The names of diverse gentlemen of vallue and habelletie to serve sum in one function and sum in another, placed hear according to their habitactions. Sr. Robart Wingefeld. Sr. Owen Hopton [struck out] Sr. William Walgrave. Sr Philipp Parker. Sr. William Springe. Sr. Robart Jermin. Sr Thomas Barneston. Sr. John Higham. Sr. Nicholas Bacon. Sr. Charles Framingham. Sr. Robert Southwell [struck out]. Nathaniel Bacon. Sr. Clement Hygham. Sr. Tho Jermin."

Here follows an extract from "The Boke of Reme'brance blongyng unto me Thomas Kytson of London mercer made the 20th days in Sept, an'o d'ni 1529". He built Hengrave Hall in 1538.

From 1592 to 1598
57 lb of butter to the Farm.
Pease spent in Homestead 4 coombe 2 bs.
Barley used in my Ladye her stillhouse 3 bs.
Wheat spent for fyrmetye in Xmas I pte.
Wheat del for the brewing of strong beere I co: 1598 an.
Haberdyngs or saltfishes.
Bullocks at Plow 3.
Eggs 415 at 11s 5d, — about 3 a penny.
Wheat to feede quailes Pheasants and Partridges.
Hoppes 30 lb at 3d a lb — Spent for the brewing of 71 comb of mault 87 lb of Hopps.

Seacoles 40 bush to the chalder.
Tallow 3d the lb.
Candles 4d the lb.
Wheat at 8s 6d the comb.
Weatherhoggs 100 at 33£.
Rye 16 comb lbz sown on 33 acres of ground. Myslen 20 comb sown on 40 acres.

5

Cardinal Wolsey

... Wolsey, that once trod the ways of glory,
And sounded all the depths and shoals of honour.

It is rather remarkable to realise that Suffolk produced one
of the greatest men of this country: Thomas Wolsey, born
in the parish of St Nicholas, Ipswich in 1471, of, it is said,
a poor father who was a butcher. It is more probable that
the father was also an affluent cattle dealer, although the
many references to the family classes them as butchers and
innkeepers. Be that as it may, Robert his father saw to it
that Thomas had a good education because he was sent to
Magdalen College, Oxford at the age of eleven, and had
graduated as Bachelor of Arts four years later. From this he
gained the sobriquet of the 'Boy Bachelor'. An interesting
summary of his life is given by Fuller in his *Worthies*:

Thomas Wolsey was born in the town of Ipswich, where a butcher,
a very honest man was his father, though a poet be thus pleased
to descant thereon:
   Brave priest, whoever was thy sire by kind
   Wolsey of Ipswich ne'er begat thy mind.
   One of so vast undertakings, that our whole book will not
afford room enough for his character; the writing whereof I
commend to some eminent person of his foundation of Christ-
church in Oxford.
   He was made Cardinal of St Cecily, and died heart-broken with
grief at Leicester 1530, without any monument, which made a
great wit of his own college thus lately complain:
   And though for his own store Wolsey might have
   A palace, or a college for his grave,
   Yet here he lies interrd, as if all
   Of him to be remembered were his fall.
   Nothing but earth to earth, nor pompous weight

45

Upon him but a pebble or a quoit,
If thou art thus neglected, what shall we
Hope after death, that are but shreds of thee?
This may be truly said of him, he was not guilty of mischevious
pride; and was generally commended for doing justice, when
chancellor of England.

He became a Fellow of his college, and in 1506 chaplain
and secretary to Fox, Bishop of Winchester. On the death of
Henry VII, he became a royal chaplain and a favourite of
Henry VIII; and from favourite to minister. His policy was
that of keeping England out of war. He visited the Low
Countries on a diplomatic errand in 1508, was rewarded with
the See of Lincoln, and in 1514 was made Archbishop of
York. In 1515 he was appointed Chancellor and became a
cardinal. He even aimed at the Papacy, a position he narrowly
missed on two occasions. His foreign policy gave England a
high place in European affairs, but at home he created a royal
despotism. This is what J.R. Green the historian says of him:

All authority was concentrated in the hands of a single minister. The
whole direction of home and foreign affairs rested with Wolsey
alone; as Chancellor he stood at the heart of public justice; his
elevation to the office of Legate rendered him supreme in the
Church. Enormous was the mass of work which he undertook, it was
thoroughly done; his administration of the Royal treasury was
economical; the number of his despatches is hardly less remarkable
than the care he bestowed upon each; as Chancellor, even More — his
avowed enemy — confesses that he surpassed all men's expectations.
The Court of Chancery, indeed, became so crowded with business
through the character for expedition and justice which it acquired
under his rule, that the subordinate courts — one of which, that of
the Master of the Rolls, still remains — had to be created for its
relief. It was this vast concentration of all secular and ecclesiastical
power in a single hand which accustomed England to the personal
government which began with Henry VIII; and it was above all,
Wolsey's long tenure of the whole Papal authority within the realm,
and the consequent suspensions of the appeals to Rome, that led
men to acquiesce at a later time in Henry's religious supremacy. For
great as was Wolsey's pride, he regarded himself and proclaimed
himself simply the creature of the King. Henry munificently

rewarded his services to the crown. He had been raised to the See of Lincoln and the Archbishopric of York, the revenue of two other Sees whose tenants were foreigners were in his hands. He was Bishop of Winchester and Abbot of St Albans, he was in receipt of pensions from France and Spain, while his official emoluments were enormous. His ambition was glutted at last with the rank of Cardinal. His pomp was almost royal. A train of prelates and nobles followed him wherever he moved; his household was comprised of five hundred persons of noble birth, and his chief posts were held by knights and barons of the realm. He spent his vast wealth with princely ostentation.

Turning back to Fuller in his *Church History*:

At this time, though Henry wore the sword, cardinal Wolsey bore the stroke all over the land; being Legate, by virtue whereof he visited all churches and religious houses . . .

And now the cardinal was busied in building his college, consisting of several courts, whereof the principal is so fair and large, it would have equalled any prince's palace, if finished according to his design; all the chambers and other offices being intended suitable to the magnificent hall and kitchen therein.

Indeed, nothing mean could enter this man's mind; but of all things, his structures were stately. He was the best harbinger that ever king Henry had, not only taking up beforehand, but building up, beautiful houses for his entertainments; which, when finished (as Whitehall, Hampton Court &c), he either freely gave them to the king, or exchanged them on very reasonable considerations.

Some say, he intended this his college to be an university in an university, so that it should have therein by itself professors of all arts, and sciences. But we may believe, that all these go by the guess, as not knowing the cardinal's mind (who knew not his own), daily embracing new designs of magnificence, on the emergency of every occasion.

This college did thrice change its name in seven years, accounting it no small credit thereunto, that it always ascended and was advanced in every alteration: First, called Cardinal's College; Then, King's College: And, at last, Christ's Church, which it retains at this day.

It was indeed to be a seat of the 'New Learning.'

In order to honour his native town, Wolsey decided to build a college at Ipswich, to serve as a nursery for his college at Oxford. The patent for this is dated 1529. The first stone was laid by John Longland, bishop of Lincoln, who was confessor to Henry VIII and the first Dean was William Capon. It was built on the grounds of the Priory of Saints Peter and Paul, which had been suppressed for the purpose.

No description of the collegiate school appears to have survived, save that it was "sumptious to behold". The site occupied six acres, and some idea of the magnificence of the building can be gauged by a letter sent to Wolsey from Capon the Dean: "We have received of Mr Dawndy [a merchant of Ipswich and a relative of the Cardinal], 171 tons of cane [Caen] stone, and within a fortnight next after Michaelmas now next coming we shall have one hundred tons more. So that your workmen shall not be unoccupied for want of stone. And the said Mr Daundy hath promised to me, that before Easter next coming we shall have here ready 1,000 tons of the said cane stone."

Wolsey was no mean scholar and it was his determination, that for both his school and his more splendid establishment at Oxford, a new plan should be introduced, in which the classics should be more prominent than those "absurb sciences which tended not to make a man learned, but merely pedantic, pert, or ostentacious and shallow". He wrote a Latin preface to Lily's *Grammar*, then lately published, which he wished taught at Ipswich. Lily was the first headmaster of St Paul's School.

He took medical knowledge under his wing. When the Royal College of Physcians was formed under Thomas Linacre, the design was patronised by Wolsey. The King granted a charter in 1518, forming the body into a community and perpetual college, and by which, among other things, power was granted them to practise as physicians in London and seven miles round. The establishment of this proved the dawn of judicious medical science and practice.

It has been suggested that the Ipswich college was destroyed by orders from Henry, after the Cardinal's fall,

The brasses of Sir Robert de Bures and Dame Alice de Bryene

Wolsey Gate

"with a malicious ferocity, highly to be deprecated, scattered the possessions of Ipswich College into the hands of divers persons, and broke up the establishment for ever".

Wodderspoon goes on: "Perhaps it was his desire that all remembrance of its illustrious townsman should be blotted out from the place of his birth. It was the wish and act of a tyrant."

The only remaining portion of this college is the gateway built of red brick, with a square stone above bearing the Royal Arms of Henry. This led to the courtyard. A public meeting held in 1919 under the chairmanship of Prince Frederick Duleep Singh posed the question of what to do with it? They decided to leave it alone. This is the only memorial left to honour the memory of Wolsey in his native town.

It is said that he suppressed, with the aid of the Pope, no less than forty small monasteries, turning out their inhabitants from house and home, for the support of these two colleges. But as Fuller wrote: "Plead not in the cardinal's case that the Houses by him suppressed were of small value; it being as great, yes, greater sacrilege to invade the widow's mite, than the large gifts which the rich priests cast into *corban*; because their bounties were but superfluous wens, whilst hers were an essential limb".

Wolsey was with Henry at the Field of the Cloth of Gold, pursuing his plans for the advancement of his country.

Wolsey's downfall came about by Henry's frantic efforts to father a son. Catherine of Aragon, whom he had married, was the widow of Arthur, Henry's elder brother, and because of the Queen's failure to produce a son through many miscarriages, he suddenly had twinges of conscience about the validity of the marriage, and sought means to rid himself of her. Wolsey agreed to this because he saw a possible alliance with France, assuming Henry would marry Margaret, Duchess of Alencon, sister to Francis, King of France. The appeal made on her knees by Catherine, as recorded by Speed, is surely classic in its quality.

Sir, — I desire to take some pity upon me, and do me justice, and right: I am a poor woman, a stranger, born out of your dominions, having here no indifferent counsellor, and less assurance of friendship. Alas! wherein have I offended, or what cause of displeasure have I given, that you intend thus to put me away? I take God as my judge, I have been to you a true and humble wife, ever conformable to your will and pleasure, never gainsaying anything wherein you took delight, without all grudge or discontented countenance; I have loved all them that loved you, howsoever their affections have been to me-ward; I have borne you children and been your wife now this twenty years. Of my virginity and marriage-bed I make God and your own conscience the judge; and if it otherwise be found, I am content to be put from you with shame. The king your father in his time for wisdom was known to be a second to Solomon; and Ferdinand of Spain, my father accounted the wisest among their kings. Could they in this match be so far overseen? Surely, it seemeth wonderful to me, that after twenty years, should be thus called in question, with new inventions against me who never intended but honesty. Alas! sir, I see I am wronged, having no counsel to speak for me, but such as are your subjects, and cannot be indifferent upon my part. Therefore, I must humbly beseach you, even in charity, to stay this course until I have advice and counsel from Spain; if not, your Grace's pleasure be done.

It is not necessary to say that this plea was of no avail.

The case put before the ecclesiastical courts to annul the marriage dragged on for too long to satisfy the King's appetite, and Wolsey was blamed in that he had lost heart when he knew that his scheme was not to be achieved. As a consequence he lost favour with both sides, the King and the Queen, and on a pretext he was banished to Esher. This was a house belonging to his bishopric of Winchester. He was here for weeks "without beds, sheets, table-cloths, cups and dishes", until he had an attack of dropsy, when the King allowed him to be moved to Richmond. A temporary restoration to power was granted, but his end was near, to be brought about largely by a Norfolk woman, who was often in Suffolk, whom the King favoured for her looks and person — Anne Boleyn. She too hated the ageing Wolsey for her own personal reasons. He had obliged the King by putting an end to Anne's secret engagement to Henry Percy, Earl of Northumberland, for which she never forgave him. In fact she had said that if it was ever in her power she would "work the Cardinal much displeasure".

The end of Wolsey was replete with pathos. He was charged with high treason through the jealousy of his rivals, of whom he had many, and was ordered to the Tower, for a transgression of the Statute of Praemunire, by holding his court as legate within the realm. (Praemunire was the offence of disregard or contempt of the king and his government, especially the offence of introducing papal or other foreign authority into England). He was already a broken man, largely through his own labours. As he was being conducted southwards an attack of dysentery forced him to rest at the Abbey of Leicester, where he made his famous apologia when he was met at the gate by the brethren: "I am come to lay my bones among you." He was ill for three days and died with this famous confession on his lips. "And, Master Kyngton, had I but served God as diligently as I have served my King, he would not have given me over in my grey hairs." His dirge was written by Shakespeare:

> Farewell! a long farewell, to all my greatness!
> This is the state of man: to-day he puts forth
> The tender leaves of hope; tomorrow blossoms,
> And bears his blushing honours thick upon him;
> The third day comes a frost, a killing frost;
> And, when he thinks, good easy man, full surely
> His greatness is a-ripening, nips his root,
> And then he falls as I do. I have ventur'd
> Like little wanton boys that swim on bladders,
> This many summers in a sea of glory,
> But far beyond my depth: my high blown pride
> At length broke under me, and now has left me
> Weary and old with service, to the mercy
> Of a rude stream that must for ever hide me.
> Vain pomp and glory of this world, I hate ye:
> I feel my heart new open'd. O how wretched
> Is that poor man that hangs on princes' favours!
> There is, betwixt that smile we would aspire to,
> That sweet aspect of princes, and their ruin,
> More pangs and fears than wars or women have;
> And when he falls, he falls like Lucifer,
> Never to hope again.

A life of Wolsey was written by one of his retainers, who was described as an Honest Suffolk man, George Cavendish of Glemsford. He has been identified as a member of the Cavendish family, mercers and drapers of London, a branch of which became later the Devonshire family. This work was in manuscript only, but several copies were made. It so remained until 1641, when a garbled version appeared by a William Sheares.

A scholarly modern edition of *The Life and Death of Cardinal Wolsey* by George Cavendish, edited by Richard S. Sylveter, was published for the Early English Text Society by the Oxford University Press in 1959. The editor there states that chronicles like Stowe, Holinshed and Speed drew largely from the manuscript, but the autograph version was not discovered until the early part of the nineteenth century, when S.W. Singer "made what has been to this day the only attempt to produce a scholarly edition".

It is evident that Cavendish gave an eye-witness account, because of his recording of the Percy-Anne episode (he spoke of Anne as the "nyght Crowe"). But some of the information came from outside, and some from Wolsey himself, recounting earlier events when they were together at Richmond. As Cavendish naively says: "To write the life and doynges of this Cardinal, it were a great works."

The prologue sets the tune: "Me seems it were no wisdom to credit every light tale, blazed by a blasphemous mouth of rude commonalty, for we daily hear how with their blasphemous trompe they spread about innumerable lies without either shame or honesty (which prima facie) sheweth forth a visage of truth, as though it were perfect veritie, matter in Deede, wherein there is nothing more untrue."

R.S. Sylvester points out that whether or not Cavendish kept a record of events cannot now be determined. But suggests he had a Renaissance eye for details of the splendid clothing and for scenes of pomp and luxury, so beloved by the Tudors. In any case it is the information in his chronicle, considered so reliable as to provide later writers with material for their studies, such as that by A.F. Pollard.

After the fall, Cavendish refused any further royal prefer-
ments and spent his later years on his Suffolk estates at
Glemsford and Cavendish.

6

An Old Manor House

Praising what is lost
  Makes the remembrance dear.

Perhaps it would be appropriate to give a description of an
old country house as lived in in the days of Mary Tudor, such
as given of Hawstead Place by Sir John Cullum. It was visited
by Queen Elizabeth I in 1578 on her progress through West
Suffolk. It is described as being moated, on an eminence,
gently sloping towards the south. Whilst there Elizabeth
dropped, into the moat, a silver-handled fan which was
retrieved by her host.

The whole range of buildings formed a courtyard, three of
the sides consisting of barns, stable, mill house, slaughter
house, blacksmith's shop, and various other offices. The
entrance was by a gatehouse in the centre of the south side,
over which were chambers for carters. The mansion house
which was also a quadrangle formed the south side, standing
higher than the other buildings and separate from them by a
wide moat, faced with bricks, and surrounded by a terrace.
The approach was by a flight of steps and a brick bridge of
three arches, through a small 'jealous' wicket, formed in the
great well-timbered gate that grated on its hinges.

"Immediately on your peeping through the wicket, the first
object that unavoidably struck you, was a stone figure of
Hercules, holding in one hand a club across his shoulders the
other resting on his hips, discharging a perennial stream of
water by the urinary passage into a carved stone bason." This
was evidently placed there for the royal visit, though, Sir
John reminds us, "Modern times would scarcely devise such a
piece of Sculpture as an amusing spectacle for a virgin

princess." The walls of the inner court were hung with an ancient pyracanthus.

Sir John now suggests we should "creep" through the wicket gate, and leads us to a door in the gateway, on the right of which leads to a small apartment known as the smoking room. He reminds us that "there is scarcely an old house without a room of this denomination. Gentlemen then had but few amusements and such a room was much in use." Mr Hervey, afterwards Earl of Bristol, writing to Mr Thomas Cullum in 1688; "desired to be remembered by the witty smoakers of Hausted".

Adjoining was a large wood closet and a passage that led to the dining room where was a large buffet. At the end of the dining room was originally a cloister, or arcade fronting east, looking into a flower garden within the walls of the moat. The arches were afterwards closed up and glazed and a parlour made at one end. Sir John comments: "There are few of these old mansions without one or more of these sheltered walking places; and they certainly had their uses: but the age of list, sandbags and carpet that dreads every breath of air, as if there were a pestilence, shudders at the idea of such a body of the element being admitted into any part of a dwelling." (We shall meet Sir John's love of fresh air again in his note about the church.) The cloisters led to the kitchen.

On the left hand of the entrance, opposite the smoking room, was the chapel, "much affected by the old manorial lords, who seem to have disdained attending the parochial church". It was last used to christen Sir John. Through this was a door into the drawing room or largest parlour and adjoining was a large gloomy hall, at the end of which was a screen of brown wainscoat, in which was a door that led to the buttery. Beneath these apartments were the cellars of vaulted brick. A staircase from the hall led to the royal apartments.

Here follows a rather nice little touch, because on this staircase, against the wall, were painted boards, representing various domestic servants. Sir John had his eye on one, "a very pretty well-painted female, said to be for a house keeper". On this floor also was the still room — "where the ladies of old much amused themselves in distilling waters and cordials, as well for the use of themselves and of their poor neighbours, as for several purposes of cooking". Ominously enough, in this room stood a death's head. A list is appended of some of the plants that might have been distilled, gathered from the Northumberland Household Book, one of the most celebrated of these records: roses, borage, fumitory, brakes, columbines, oak leaves, hart's tongue, parsley, balm, walnut leaves, ox-tongue, primroses, sage, sorrel, red mint, betony, cowslip, dandelion, fennel, scabias, elder flowers, marigolds, wild tansy, wormwood, woodbine, endive, haws.

It might be interesting in passing to note the quality of some of these flowers. The rose was the queen of all flowers, particularly as Suffolk produced its own Burnet-leaved variety, known as the Dunwich rose, Anne Pratt reminds us that in former days, when garlands were hung in churches, in order to "attemper the aire, coole and made freshe the places, to the delight and comfort of such as are therein", the rose was usually chosen for the purpose. It was used medicinally — the hips made a homely conserve with sugar — and not least as a perfume, for who has not heard of attar of roses. Oil of rose, to be distilled from the White Damask rose, was a sovereign remedy for sore eyes.

And is not the grave of the gentle FitzGerald adorned with Persian roses to remind us of his *Rubaiyat*. When my mother lost two little children, she had a china rose planted on the grave to remind her of her young days in Suffolk where the children might have called the hips and haws Cat-hips.

Borage, used to grow in cottage gardens. According to Burton,

> Borage and Hellebore fill two scenes,
> Sovereign plants to purge the veins
> Of melancholy, and clear the heart
> Of those black fumes which make it smart.

Fumitory. Its young tops were prepared as a tonic. It was
to be found by the roadsides and cornfields. Clare sings of it:

> And Fumitory too, a name
> Which Superstition holds to fame,
> Whose red and purple mottled flowers
> Are cropp'd by maids in weeding hours,
> To boil in water, milk and whey,
> For washes on a holiday,
> To make their beauty fair and sleek,
> And scare the tan from summer's cheek;
> And oft the dame will feel inclined,
> As childhood's memory comes to mind,
> To turn her hook away, and spare
> The blooms it loved to gather there.

Brake is bracken. The root of the male fern was a specific
against the tape-worm. The English name columbine, derived
from a fanciful likeness to a dove. This is produced if one
petal is separated from the flower cluster. It was also known
as the water carrier because the leaves collect water in their
hollow, and was the insignia of a deserted lover.

> The Columbine by lonely wand'rer taken,
> Is then ascribed to such as are forsaken.

Hart's tongue is a fern. Parsley is used in the kitchen. Balm
is balsam, the common name of certain succulent herbaceous
plants from which ointment is derived for healing purposes.
Ox-tongue is hawksweed, a bright yellow flower that grows
by hedgerows and roadsides, and has very slight medicinal
properties. In old times it was familiarly called yellow
succory and yellow ox-tongue. Sage is salvia, used for
flavouring meats.

Sorrel is a plant with small red flowers. Sometimes boiled
as spinach, or used to flavour salads and soups. The root is
very astringent and was considered to possess valuable
medicinal properties. When dried and boiled it yields a good
red dye.

Red Mint is probably Peppermint. Betony is a common

plant of the hedgerow, of great repute in ancient and medieval medicine. It is used as a yellow dye for wood. Dandelion is the 'Sunflower of the Spring' also the school-boy's clock in every town. Its root is chiefly valuable as a remedy for long-standing liver complaints. Sliced and boiled, the decoction will, if persevered with as a medicine, prove an excellent tonic, and will clear the complexion far better than any cosmetic. The dose is from one ounce to four, two or three times a day.

Fennel is found on sea cliffs from Norfolk downwards. The seeds are carminative and are (or were) employed in medicine. The leaves are sometimes used for cooking. Its old name was ragged lady. Scabia is a plant formerly thought of use in scurvy eruptions, or itchiness. Elder flowers are used for making distilled water, which is cooling and refreshing. The plant had considerable medicinal value. The undeveloped buds, when picked, formed a good substitute for capers. The berries are used for wine.

The marigolds referred to were probably marsh marigolds, difficult to distinguish from the buttercup. In common with most acrid and poisonous plants it possesses a certain old medical reputation. One doctor believed in the exhalation of some potent qualities from the flowers because a girl was cured of fits by the placing of a quantity of the flowers in her bedroom. This incident induced some to make an infusion of the plant and administer it to children as a cure for various kinds of fits. It was also called water calthrops and meadow rout. Mrs Lancaster who wrote on flowers, believed that Shakespeare had this in mind when he wrote:

> Hark! hark, the lark at heaven's gate sings,
>   And Phoebus 'gins to rise,
> His steeds to water at those springs,
>   On chaliced flowers that lies.

Wild tansy is common on hedge banks and waste places. It used to be collected by country folk to make tansy wine, which was thought to have certain valuable remedial effects.

It was made into cakes and puddings to be eaten during Lent because of its bitter taste. It flowers during August and September with clusters of yellow button-like blossoms with a powerful aromatic odour.

Wormwood is a wild flower found in waste places. Skeat says it should be ware-wood or mind preserver but its name was probably given because it was used as a remedy for worms. It is a powerful little stomachic and tonic used in dyspepsia and to flavour drinks.

Woodbine, or honeysuckle, is also called the goat-leaf. Shakespeare said:

> So doth the woodbine, the sweet honeysuckle
> Gently entwist the maple.

Endive is a composite plant with a head of pale blue flowers. The leaves after being blanched to dimish their bitterness are used in salads and stews. Haws are the fruit of the hawthorn.

Returning to Hawstead Place, next to one of the bed-chambers (all upper rooms were designated chambers), was a wainscoted closet, seven feet square with panels painted with various sentences, emblems and mottoes. The dresses of the figures dating from James I. Here is a list:

1 A monkey sitting in a house window and scattering money in the street.
2 A camel trampling in dirty water.
3 A fire on the bank of a river.
4 A painter, having begun to sketch out a female portrait.
5 A human tongue, with bat's wings, and a scaly contorted tail, mounting into the air.
6 A tree with sickly leaves, and a honey-comb at its roots. Near is another, quite leafless.
7 An eagle in the air with an elephant in its talons.
8 Some trees leafless and torn up by the roots; with a confused landscape. Above, the sun and a rainbow.
9 An old man asleep, with asses ears, and ants that seem carrying something into his mouth.

10 One man standing on the uppermost point of the earth; and another antipodal to him.

11 A man endeavouring to light a candle at a glow worm. [What a lovely little conceit.]

12 A globe resting on a crab.

13 A greyhound disengaged from his collar, and licking his master's hand.

14 The sun quite black and golden stars.

15 A blackamore smoking a pipe.

16 A bird of prey, in the air, devouring a small bird.

17 A man rowing in a boat, with a town close in sight.

18 A bee-hive, with bees about it.

19 A fire bursting from the top of a chimney.

20 A pilgrim traversing the earth; with a staff, and a light-coloured hat, with a cockle shell on it.

21 A man's hand holding something like a rope lighted, and from which smoke and fire issue.

22 An ass standing on his hind legs, his head appearing through the upper part of a white area. Beneath his head a horse is feeding. Near them is a woodcock, with one foot on a lanthorn.

23 A bear in his den.

24 A man taking the dimensions of his own forehead with a pair of compasses.

25 A man in a fool's dress, blowing with a pair of bellows a pot suspended in the air, with some fire in it.

26 A death's head, with some plant of a dark hue issuing from one eye, and lying on the ground; while a similar plant, of a verdant colouring, springs erect from the other.

27 A bat flying after a large black insect.

28 A rose and a poppy.

29 A mermaid, holding a mirror in one hand, and combing her hair with the other.

30 A bucket descending into a well.

31 An eagle, going to take something from a fire. Her nest of young ones near.

32 A naked blackamore pointing to a swan with one hand, and to his own teeth with the other.

33 A bird thrusting its head into an oyster, partly open.

34 A bird feeding in a crocodile's mouth.

35 A boar trampling on roses.

36 A ship that has anchored on a whale, which is in motion. The crew alarmed.

37 Two rams fighting, detached from the flock.

38 A hedgehog rolled up, with apples on its prickles.

39 A philosopher looking at a star with a quadrant.

40 A garland of leaves lying on the ground, and in flames.

41 A full bucket drawn up to the top of a well.

The bottom panels are adorned with flowers in a good taste.

Here then was a mixture of Hakluyt and Drake's voyage round the world in 1590, built into one's own home, a package tour as a precurser of our age. It may be there is a connection here with the Gate House at West Stow, where in an upper room are wall paintings depicting the Seven Ages of Man, possibly by the same artist. That Hall has been associated with Mary Tudor because her arms are on the front of the Gate House.

Sir John goes on to say the windows were spacious and high, that the walls were of wood and plaster, presumably oak studs, and the roof was evidently of tiles, with good overhangs. In 1685 they paid taxes for thirty-four hearths. That lovely old house had probably stood on the same site as used at the Norman conquest, a manor with "cartiloges and gardens pidgeon houses and windmills".

Like to Acton and Westhorpe, Hawstead Manor became a farmhouse and this idyllic self-contained settlement vanished. But as a village even when it passed into the hands of the Cullum family — one of whom amassed a fortune as a draper in London, became a baronet and purchased the estate — it rejoiced in a village green or common of no less than twenty-four acres. Moreover, it was surrounded by some of the best farming land in Suffolk.

Apparently the church was consumed by a dreadful fire in 1666, and this memorial went with it:

Here under resteth the body of the truly vertuous gentlewomen Mrs Marie Cullum, daughter of Mr Nicholas Crispe, merchant, wife of Thomas Cullum draper of this parish. She departed this life the 22nd of July, 1637, in the 36th year of her age, having had issue 5 sons and 6 daughters.
> If that all women were but near as good as she,
> Then all men surely might in wives right happy be.
> Would any know, how virtus rare in her did take;
> I say no more; she was a Crisp, born of a Pake.

It appears that the first of the family connected with Hawstead, was Thomas Cullum, who, being a younger son, was put to business in London, and became a very successful draper in Gracechurch Street. One of the former owners was Sir William Drury, one of the Suffolk gentlemen who espoused the cause of Queen Mary (Bloody Mary), joining her at Kenninghall.

THOMAS SECKFORD, Efq^r

Founded the   Alms-Houfes

in Woodbridge,   Anno Domini

15   87.

(*left*) The helmet of
the third Duke of
Norfolk;   (*right*)
Thomas Seckford

Seckford's almshouses at Woodbridge, 1792

Seckford Hall, 1791

7

Neighbours

People will not look forward to posterity, who never look backward to their ancestors.

We might now look at one or two of the neighbours of these old manor houses, from a list provided for us by S.H.A. Hervey in his *Green Book of Weststow and Wordwell*; and particularly at his rather naive way of telling the tale.

First comes the Lucas family, whose pedigree seems to have been meticulously traced before surnames were provided. This family was associated with West Stow down to the time of the War of the Roses. A question mark hangs over them from the start, as the Reverend Mr Hervey points out: "As we start with a man who was born within a hundred years of the Norman Conquest of England, when Normans and Saxons were living still separate and not yet welded into one nation, it seems natural to ask, To whether of the twain did he belong? Was he a dominating Norman or a dominated Saxon? Had his father been in the land for ten generations before him, or had his grandfather come over and fought at Hastings in the ranks of the Normans?" In any case these Lucases were servants of the Crown. They also belonged to Little Saxham, Horringer and other places, so they must have been very acceptable neighbours.

Next come the Crofts family, a name derived, as the reverend gentleman reminds us, from a croft or small enclosed field near a house. He also suggests that the S was subsequently tacked on to suit the convenience of the tongue. Apparently the East Anglian mouth needs that letter more than the northern and western tongues, as in Yorkshire and Herefordshire the name is still Croft.

S.H.A.H. continues: "The history of the Crofts family is much like that of the Lucas family. In each case we see the earliest generations settled in Bury St Edmunds. Each with bag and baggage passed out of Bury by the north gate to take up its abode at West Stow. Each moved from West Stow to Little Saxham. Each eventually moved out of Suffolk altogether. In all these moves the Lucas's went first, the Crofts followed after. Each enjoyed the favour of Tudor princes, each profited by the fall of Bury abbey."

Of the eight generations, John, son and heir of Thomas Crofts he says: "His annals, his children's names and fortunes, behold they are all written in the little Saxham volume . . . His portrait painted in 1612 is somewhere. I know not where." A recent descendant must have been Ernest Crofts, R.A., who ended his days at Blythburgh, in the church of which is a memorial to him.

Sir Henry Crofts who saw service in Ireland as a soldier was buried in old St Paul's, with this inscription as given by Dugdale:

> Six lines this image shall delineate,
> 　Hight Croft, high borne, in spirit and vertue high,
> Approv'd, belov'd, a Knight, stout Mars his mate,
> 　Love's fire, war's flame, in heart, head, hand and eye;
> Which flame, war's comet, grace now so refines,
> 　That fixt in Heaven, in Heaven and Earth it shines.

Now follows Edward Proger, who instead of the East Anglian Crofts was a Welshman by race, a Londoner by birth and a courtier by profession. "A bed-chamber man: not born to a farthing." He was a faithful Carolean and this is what was said of him: "The quality of loyalty and fidelity in Edward Proger was tried and proved. To be loyal to a prince who has grants and pensions and rewards and titles to fling about him is one thing: it is loyalty untried and so unproved. To be loyal to a prince who through fifteen years is in poverty and exile, with a price upon his head and scarce a penny in his pocket, is another thing: it is loyalty tried and proved."

He died aged ninety-two and had lived in the reigns of all the Stuart rulers and had been intimate with most of them. Born in the reign of James I, he died in the last year of Queen Anne, 1713, the last day of the year and that of his life. Had he lived a little longer he would have seen the House of Hanover on the throne.

West Stow Hall passed to his daughter Catherine, and a tablet to her memory in Hampton Church, Middlesex is not without interest:

To the ever dear memory of Mrs Catherine Proger, who departed this life at her seat at West Stow hall in Suffolk, March 2, 1736, and lies near this place in her father's vault. She was daughter and one of the co-heiresses of the honourable Edward Proger, Esq, late ranger of Middle park, now called Bushy Park, who was descended from the Progers of Gwerndee in Monmouthshire, was Page of honour to king Charles the first; Groom of the Bedchamber to King Charles the second, and 17 years Member of Parliament for Brecknockshire, who was born June 16, 1621 and dy'd Dec. 31, 1713.

This monument was erected by Sir Sydenham Fowke and Dame Frances his wife, as a small acknowledgement to so good a father and so affectionate a sister.

Thus enters the Fowke family because in the death of Catherine Proger West Stow came to her youngest sister, Frances, who was baptised at Hampton on 11th March, 1677. She was married on 30th December 1721 to Major Sydenham Fowke at West Stow and took up residence there where she lived twenty-two years as a wife and nine as a widow. This brings us down to the times of the Cornwallisses, the Graftons, the Cullums and the Bristol family.

On the death of Frances, Lady Fowke, in 1752, West Stow passed to her nephew, John Edwards. He had at the same time to add to his name, and thus became — John Progers Herbert Edwards. Within half a century West Stow became part of the Culford Estate, ceased to be a hall and became a farmhouse.

8

Butley Priory

Bishop, and abbot, and prior were there;
Many a monk, and many a friar,
Many a knight and many a squire.

Barham

Let us look for a moment at Butley Priory, surely one of the most beautiful of the religious houses of Suffolk, set in shepherds' country in peaceful seclusion. There can be no wonder that Mary Tudor found it a delightful and welcome retreat from the court life to which she had been used, where she could be herself rather than a pawn of political intrigue.

It was founded in 1171 by a great Suffolk man, Ranulf de Glanvill, who was soon to become Justiciar, or chief minister, to Henry II. He followed Coeur de Lion to the Holy Land. He also drew out a codification of the laws of England, for which lawyers and historians have expressed both admiration and gratitude. He was already a substantial landowner in the county, and the sandy land on which he established the priory was part of the marriage portion of his wife, Bertha, daughter of Theobald of Valoins, Lord of Parham. The priory was well endowed within a century of its birth, by sixteen churches and sixty other buildings in the county, which placed it amongst the most substantial houses in East Anglia.

The first prior was Gilbert (1171-95), of whom little is known. He was succeeded by William (c1195-1213). His name occurs in a charter by which he and the convent granted to the Priory of Woodbridge the tithes of Baldwin's Mill in Woodbridge. On 9th March 1235, King Henry III paid a visit to Butley. By this time the founder's property had passed on his death to his three daughters, the eldest of whom, Matilda, received the Manor of Benhall and the advowson of Butley Priory. Her husband, William de Auberville, was a substantial benefactor and he is alleged to have repaired or even rebuilt the priory. Coming down the years, a Prior Thomas entertained Archbishop Peckham, who was also a benefactor.

Edward I's royal policy of billeting superannuated servants on monasteries is well illustrated at Butley. In April 1303 Roger le Usher was sent to be maintained at the convent with two horses and two grooms. He was evidently accepted as an unwelcome guest. In June, Master William le Surigien arrived with horse and groom. However, the Canons sent him back with the excuse that the house was so burdened with debts, or by the inundation of the sea, that they were unable to fulfil the King's prayers. The reference to the sea is most interesting as showing the difficulties that the coastline was experiencing, together with Dunwich. But the King did not accept the excuses, and William was back, and there he remained until his death, which occured before March 1312.

A Prior William de Geytone succeeded in 1311. He was to prove one of the great priors of the House. In all probability it was during his period of office that the noble gatehouse was built, which is the only survivor of this splendid priory. His fine tombstone, adorned with his brass, was in the church, or the chapter house of the priory. It still exists, but is now in Holllesly Church, shorn of its brass. (The only other man of prominence to whom tradition assigns a grave at Butley is Michael de le Pole, third Earl of Suffolk, who fell at Agincourt. But he may have been buried at Ewelme, Oxfordshire.)

Next to the building of the gatehouse the most important event during William's priorate was his presidency, along with the Prior of Dunstable, at the General Chapter of the Augustinian Order in the Province of Canterbury, which took place at Northampton in 1325. William died about 1332, and was succeeded by Alexander de Stratford. How the inmates got on during the Black Death is not known, but the Prior, Matthew, survived it, although he appears to have been in failing health.

It is interesting to notice the local names of some of the priors and canons. For example there was a Matthew de Pakenham, John de Framelingham, Gilbert of Dedham, Alexander de Drenkeston, William de Halesworth, John Debenham. This is a foil against the suggestion that these positions were filled by men from the Continent.

With the election of William de Halesworth (1374-1410) Butley entered upon a period of long tenures, the rule of Halesworth and his two next successors, William Randeworth and William Poley, covering 109 years. The latter (1444-83) received his confirmation as prior when two doctors of Canon Law and John Squyers, Rector of Alderton, sat in Butley parish church to examine the formalities of the election which had taken place by acclamation. A number of legal disputes occured in his reign, the most important referred to the only benefice in the City of London belonging to them, that of St Stephen, Coleman Street. It was alleged that the advowson of this church had been acquired without licence, but it was settled in Butley's favour.

The cellarer was evidently the most important official after the subprior. He was the only official to be named, other than the prior and the subprior, at a visitation of 1514, and on the only two occasions when we are told the office previously held by a newly-elected prior, we learn that he had been cellarer, viz. William de Geytone, 1311, and Thomas Sudbourne 1528.

When we come to Robert Brenmore or Brommer (1506-9), there was a grant made by Henry VII in frankalmoin (a form of land tenure), of the Church and monastery of St Mary, Snape and its properties. This benefice, although welcomed at the time, seems to have been a bad bargain, for the Priory of Snape had previously been dependent on St John's, Colchester, and so much trouble ensued that Butley surrendered its interest the following year. Then comes the sad news that Prior Robert committed suicide early in 1509, an event without parallel in the history of the house.

Augustine Rivet's (1509-28) was a well known period of

rule, during which a Canon Reginald Westerfyld was alleged to have called the junior bretheren "horesons". He received a caution from the bishop. There was also a complaint that the choir books were out of repair. A few years later the cry was the food was bad — which was put down to the cellarer's fault — that the choir books were still out of repair, the church ruinous and the roof defective, "and it rains in the Refectory". In 1526, things were worse; there was no scholar at the university, the books and vestments were still out of repair, and "the water which used to flush and cleanse the drain in the dormitory needed reformation".

It was during Augustine's priorate that the nobility, including Mary Tudor, resorted to the priory. Staverton Park had been leased to the prior and convent for fifty years by Thomas Howard, second Duke of Norfolk, in the time of Henry VIII, and it was sold to the convent by the third Duke on 24th February 1529. This third Duke, Lord Willoughby, and others were at Butley, fox-hunting, on 16th September, 1526, and were accompanied to the chase by Prior Augustine. The Duke was at Butley again in 1527 to dinner and stayed the night, and in 1529 he came again with the Earl of Surrey, his son, and twenty-four servants. By the end of 1528 Augustine was dead. Henry Baret of Butley, "servant to Master Pryor there", left all his property to the priory and its inmates, and "for glazing and whitening of the refectory thereoff both sides, and to the making of Buttley brigge".

On 10th January 1529 a letter was despatched to Wolsey by William the Subprior, and ten other canons, the last of whom, Thomas Yppisswyche (Ipswich) wrote it, stating that they have compromitted (to entrust, to commit) the election of a prior into his hands and recommend Thomas Sudbourne, whom they had intended to elect unanimously as a "person for that office in our opynion right able and most convenyent". Wolsey therefore appointed Thomas Sudbourne or Sudbury or Manning (1529-38) to be the last prior of Butley.

In 1532 the last episcopal visitation occured, by Bishop Nicke of Norwich, when most of the old complaints cropped up again: the Infirmary is still unsatisfactorily organised; the choir books are out of repair; the food is bad; the lead roof of the presbytery is going to ruin, and that of both transepts; the ceiling of the chapter house is out of order and the refectory is so cold, especially in winter, that the brethren get gout. But the fact was that they had become a rather futile and querulous lot of old men — which, according to J.N.L. Myers (on whose history of the priory this account is based), goes far to explain the ease with which the monasteries of England were so soon to fall before the vigorous economic enterprise of the successful middle class. (Bishp Nicke, also spelt Nykke, was a cruel persecutor of all those who professed the doctrine of the Reformation, and during his episcopate Robert Adams, clerk, also Thomas Ayers, Thomas Bingy, Thomas Norrice and Thomas Bilney, priests, suffered martyrdom.)

On 1st March 1538 the house with all its lands and properties was surrendered, and the deed was signed by Thomas Manning and eight of his twelve canon in residence. A letter from William Petre, the commissioner who had received the surrender, ran: "Right Worshipful — We have to-day received the surrender of Butley, to which the Convent has assented very quietly. It is the best leaded house that I have seen. The lead is worth £1,000 but there is no other riches but cattle." From a study of local wills of the period, it has been deduced that the priory was the least popular, as it was also the richest, religious foundation in this part of Suffolk.

We now come to the gatehouse, which has been saved to us in a remarkable state of preservation, owing partly to the quality of the stone employed, partly because it became the nucleus of two domestic houses. Examination of the stone makes it probable that it was French from the Valley of the Yonne, and landed at the priory wharf, which was in a field about two hundred yards south-west of the priory church. This has long since disappeared. Although it is said that before the beginning of the nineteenth century, when the sea wall was built up the Butley river, the tide must have run right up to the priory grounds, which then abutted straight upon the tidal marshes.

The gateway, which faces north, has been described as presenting in many of its features one of the most complete and interesting monastic entrances preserved. Its famous armorial has been described as being unique in England, with no parallel in the world; and as a work of genius. This noted conception includes the Royal Arms of England, which makes it prior to 1340, when France ancient was quartered. It consists of a frieze of thirty-five shields in five rows or bands, alternating with thirty-five fleurs-de-lys panels of the same size, the priory being dedicated to the Virgin Mary. Each fleur-de-lys is carved upon a small piece of stone centred upon two rows of squared flints and the shields also project from the blocks upon which they are cut. Above many of them peeps out a quaint little bogie head or canon's portrait, and the spandrels on either side of the base point are carved into delightful grotesques. It is all an amazing fantasy.

The series of shields have been aptly described as a concise history of England at the period, traced through the great families represented, including England's association with foreign powers. All are grouped round the crucifix which occupies the central shield in the top row. The first is international and consists of the great Christian countries; second, come the chief officers of state; third, some great baronial families; four, East Anglian families; five, Suffolk families. The shields include at least five benefactors of the priory.

We might leave Butley with all its rich memories, with the lines written by a former headmaster of Winchester, Dr M.J. Rendall, who lived in the 1926 house that was created from the derelict gatehouse, and who did so much in the way of excavations with the help of an enthusiastic group of Wykehamists — this included tracing the whole of the precinct wall, which it is interesting to know was built on the local septaria, dug up from the sea.

This great Armorial cut in flint and stone
tells of the morning of a mighty nation,
whose lion scutcheon holds its proper station
hard by the Holy Cross, due service done.
Below her Barons in just order set
serenely stand as they serenely fought
for right and freedom — nothing less they sought —
de Vere and Beaumont, Bohun, Plantagenet.
This was the soul of England, honour, faith
and beauty; for amid this strict array
spring gentler things: there is an interspace
for Mary lillies. Come, the artist saith,
Play, piper, play: be glad this holy day
and sing aloud, ye knights, for Mary's grace.

Dr Montague J Rendall

9

The Registers and the Parsons

There are few places more favourable to the study of character than
an English country church.

Washington Irving

In those far-off days every little village church seemed to
have its parson, although in many cases the cures were held in
plurality, so that one does not know if the holder of the
living was in residence or not. In any case some of these
livings were rich, and Goldsmith's parson, passing rich on
forty pounds a year, must have been a rarity. As to the
clergy's erudition, this is revealed in the shocking way the
registers were kept, with great gaps and phonetic spelling.
One must give the prize to the man who could enter a burial
as "Robert Horls, widower," for Hall. However, at Halesworth on Christmas day 1594 the weather was so cold that
the rector could not thaw the ink to write down the names of
the communicants. Some entries still reflect the sadness, or
indifference, at time of the insertion, as 1591; "A beggar
whose name we do not know." That brings vividly to mind
those pathetic crosses in the First World War: "An unknown
soldier. Known unto God." Then in 1622 comes "Two infant
sonnes of John Booty, and one would like to know the
reason for the name Barbary Arnold in 1640. Was that
reminiscent of a close relative having been attacked by those
pirates? Harking back to 1556 in the will of George Fyrmage
of Icklingham comes this bequest: "Allso I gyve to John Dixe
my page ii shepe." A shepherd, he may have been farming at
Wordwell in 1566. Shepherds were highly prized in those
days, so in 1599, William Crosse servant to Nicholas Cocke,
shepherd, is entered amongst the burials. But what do you
make of such an unfortunate name as William Whalebelly,

1754.? Could this have been a case of a pious person, possibly shipwrecked and saved, inventing the name by recalling the incident in the old book?

It is, however, surprising how some of those old men, or young men possibly, shut themselves away from the world in order to study. Such was John Boyse, who was instituted June 1591 at West Stow on the death of his father. At the age of five he could read Hebrew, which his father taught him. He went to Hadleigh grammar school and then to St John's College, Cambridge. From 1584 to 1595 he was Greek lecturer at Cambridge. In 1591 he succeeded his father at West Stow, but resigned in 1593, when his mother sent him to live with her brother Poley. In 1596 he was instituted to the living at Boxworth near Cambridge, and soon afterwards married the daughter of his predecessor there. In 1604 he was appointed one of the translators of the King James' Bible. Then in 1615 he was a Prebendary of Ely, where he died in 1644 aged eighty-three.

Another of these, but of much later date, was the Reverend Professor Henslow, rector of Hitcham, and professor of botany at Cambridge. It was said of him that the interest he took in his parish schools induced him to think that the girls might with advantage know something of the plants and vegetation of their own village. With his characteristic energy and goodness, he set about teaching all who chose to learn the elements of botany, and by the encouragement of his own kindly smile and approving words, he soon succeeded in establishing a genuine love of plants, not only to look at, but to understand. He arranged for his pupils a system of naming, classifying and drying their specimens. This collection went to the educational department of the South Kensington Museum, as an example and encouragement to other village schools.

Turning to the east side of the county, I have been going through a transcript of the "Register Booke of Bramefeilde, of all the Christingngs, Weddings and Buryngs from the Feast of St Michael the Archangel being in the 30th year of King

Henry VIIIth, 1539-1586, and 1693-1889." (It should be recorded that Bramfield Church has a detached tower, and one of the finest screens in Suffolk. Then to, it has the last fragment in the hall grounds of an old oak that was a waymark when one of the Bigods was scampering off home from the wrath of his king.)

Many of the surnames are of good old Suffolk stock that still survive, in spite of all the changes that are being thrust upon us, but it is the christian names that intrigue one most. For example, in 1544 there was an "Olyff ffaro dowgter of Edmund ffaro". This suggests the Scandinavian origin of Olive in no uncertain manner.

Biblical names continue all through the years, beginning with Esdras Fforman in 1549, together with Habrah'n Waldyng, although the Old Testament never gave the great leader an aspirate. Tobbyas Fall appears in 1581, Beltiah, daughter of John Winter, in 1703; and then we come to the delightful combination of Elisha and Jehu, sons of Samuel and Hannah Cullingford in 1731. This reminds us that Elisha went to heaven in a chariot, while Jehu always drove in a great hurry. Martha in 1738 was the daughter of John Serocold, a stranger, and Ziporah appears in 1787. Now follows Esau and Bela, sons of James Crisp in 1790; with Japhet and Jeptha, twin sons of John Smith and Hall his wife. Hepizibah in 1828 and again in 1851, Jeshophat in 1843, Zipporah in 1845, Moses in 1862, and Barzillai, a servant, in 1838.

I must confess to a great liking for some of the girls' names, such as Pacyence Walpole in 1551, Patty in 1797, Parmella in 1814, Nicey in 1827. Alas Nicey only graced this world for thirteen months. Perhaps Liddy in 1831 grew up with such a pretty name and became 'Auntie Liddy'; but Eunice really belongs to the Biblical names, as does Charity. Phereby does not speak very well for the erudition of the minister. Perhaps it was the same gentleman who spelt Chertsey, Churchsey. But what do you make of a Saundry Carver in 1786? Or Philadelphia as a girl's name in 1713?

What did the folk in Bramfield know of that city of Independence?

Fees were noted for a year or two beginning in 1800, and occupations in 1813, of which labourers were chief. Others were: cordwainer, groom, butler, coachman, wheelwright, sailor, exciseman, smith, brewer and malster, engineer, railway labourer, collar maker (for horses), policeman, whitesmith, artisan, engine driver, ratcatcher (who became a vermin destroyer later on), sugar boiler, thatcher and husbandman. Then follows woodman, upholsterer, leather cutter, shepherd and brickmaker.

From which you will see that Bramfield was a tight little community, particularly so as they had a 31st November in 1766. But on 24th March 1570 Elizabeth Denny, "daughter unto John Denny, Clerk and Alles his wif", was baptised "ye . . . and being borne on ye Monday which was ye XX day of March between V and VI of ye clock in ye morning". On the margin is written "ye Sone in Aris". This was the commencement of the solar year, which is the greatest festival in Persia.

There was a bit of disturbance in church in 1570. "Memorandum that the banes of Rychard Wappoll and Rose Simson was published the VI day of August and so was asked two several sondays & ye last sonday being ye XIII day of ye same month did Thomas Neue forbid it no cause yt he could lay against him but he sayd whan I am orderly I should know." Five years later Rychard Wappoll married Alls Tomson.

We might end with two period pieces in the form of large flat stones in the chancel floor:

> Here lies the Body of Arthur Applethwaite
> Second Son of Henry Applethwaite
> of Huntingfield of this County Gent.
> (Who was Favorite and Bayliff to
> Henry Hevengingham, Henry Heron,
> and John Bence, Deceased, and remains
> so to Alexander Bence and George
> Dashwood, all Esquires, and succesively

owners of the Heveningham Hall Estate)
who died on the ninth day of September
A.D. 1733. And the 39th year of his age
   He married Bridgett the Eldest Daughter
And at length, Sole Heiress of Lambert
   Nelson, late of this Parish, Gent. By whom
he had no issue, and to whom (Having by
   his Father's Instigation made no will)
      He left her no Legacy but a Chancery-
Suit with his Eldest Brother for her
      own Paternal Estates in this Town
      and Blyford.

Between the Remains of her Brother Edward
   and of her Husband Arthur
Here lies the Body of Bridgett Applethwaite
   once Bridgett Nelson
After the Fatigues of a Married Life
   Borne by her with Incredible Patience
for Four Years and Three Quarters bating three
   weeks,
and after the Enjoinment of the Glorious
   Freedom
of an easy and Unblemisht widowhood
   For four years and upwards
She Resolved to run the Risk of a second Marriage
   bed
But Death forbad the Banns-
   and having with an Apoplectick Dart
(The same Instrument with which he had
   Formerly
Dispatcht her Mother)
   Toucht the most vital part of her Brain;
She must have fallen Directly to the Ground
   (as one Thunderstruck)
If she had not been catcht and Supported
   by her Intended Husband.
Of which Invisible Bruise

After a struggle for above sixty Hours
   With that grand enemy to Life
(But the certain and Mercifull Friend to Helpless
   Old Age)
In Terrible Convulsions Plaintive Groans or
   Stupefying Sleep
Without Recovery of her Speech or Senses
She dyed on the 12th day Sepr in ye year of our
   Lord 1737
   of her own age 44.

Coming down the years an excellent description of a church service is given by Lord Manners Hervey in *Annals of a Village*:

> Inside the church there, on the right, is Mr Wigson's pew. The seats are elevated a little above the level of the church pews, and they face the north. Mr Wigson is churchwarden, an office the most important among the old-time offices of the vestry. [There were two beadles, bearing the lovely names of Tom Orange and William Lilly]. The pews are high, the pulpit is a three-decker, and there is a gallery. The charity of those days is seen in the presence, in fixed seats, right and left, of four old men and four old women. The old men wear duffel coats, the old women red cloaks. These garments were gifts. About twelve of the older scholars of the school, too, attract the eye with their dresses (also a gift of charity) of blue or brown (in alternate years), with white tippets, crimped at the neck, white aprons and straw bonnets. The armlets short and sleeves of white calico are worn tied beneath the armlets. The children themselves plaited the straw of the bonnets and so worn, it was made into straw hats by an Ickworth woman, Mrs Race of Morterboys.

I am always glad that I was one of the last churchwardens under the old vestry system.

'Spare the rod and spoil the child' was a maxim then much practised, as in the case of a Mr Henry Boulton of Snape, born at Thorpeness in 1869. He commenced schooling at Aldringham at quite an early age. The school was kept by two maiden laides, the Misses Backhouse of Knodishall, and Henry recalled the daily visits of the local vicar, who after hearing the scripture lessons would oblige the teachers by dispensing justice in no uncertain manner to the misdoers of the previous day. Those who played truant were invested with a white card with suitable wording, and this was hung over the culprit's neck by means of a red tape, as witness of his or her misdeeds. Games and recreation were strictly forbidden and after school in summer the children ran home to assist their mother in picking stones off the fields for the award of 1½ d. a bushel.

Incidentally, in the winter the Thorpeness children did not need much persuasion to hurry home, for a ghostly hen and a brood of checks were rumored to frequent a certain field on their route. Late one evening a party of men were returning from Leiston when they thought they saw this apparition, but it later proved to be a large piece of brown paper, blown about by the wind.

10

The Bacon Family

Arms and Hatchments, Resurgam. —Here is an opportunity for moralising.

Thackeray

One of the most interesting and prolific of the Suffolk families was that of the Bacons, who had estates at Acton, Herringfleet, Gillingham, Raveningham, Baconsthorpe, Erwarton, Friston, Harleston, Hesset, Ipswich, Oulton, Redgrave and Shrubland, with others in Norfolk. They appear to have derived from one Robert Bacon of Drinkstone, who came of good yeoman stock. It was his second son, Nicholas, probably educated at the school attached to the abbey in Bury St Edmunds, who went to London and was called to the Bar in 1533, and whose rise to greatness was phenomenal. He was created Lord Keeper of the Great Seal by Queen Elizabeth, a post he held for twenty years.

At the Dissolution of the Monasteries he received large grants of the abbey lands, including Redgrave and Botesdale. At the former he built himself a house on the site of Abbot Samson's stone-built villa, where he was visited by Queen Elizabeth twice, the first time in 1559 and again in 1578 when she made her grand tour to Norwich. In 1559 she knighted "Mayster Nichola Bacon", his son, as she made her way to Brockford.

This second Sir Nicholas, who succeeded his father in 1579, added more estates to the family by marrying Anne Butts, which brought him the Butts estate at Thorneys, Norfolk, and half the Bures estate. They had a large family of nine sons and three daughters. The second of his sons, Edmund, succeeded to Redgrave. About 1686 Redgrave was sold to Lord Chief Justice Sir John Holt, who was said to have saved the life of many a poor old wretched woman when the witchcraft trials were on. Nothing now remains of the house, which was destroyed in our time, according to A.L. Rowse, and the archives were whisked away to Chicago.

In *Minutes from Nicholas Stone's Pocket Book*, 1620, is the following: "In Suffolk I made a tomb for Sir Edmund Bacon's Lady in the Church at Redgrave. I made another for his sister Lady Gawdy in the same place. I made two pictures of white marble of Sir Nicholas Bacon and his lady and they were laid upon his tomb that Bernard Jonson had made there, for which I was paid by Sir Edmund Bacon £200." (Nearby are a helmet, sword and remains of gauntlets.)

There is also a good brass to Anne Butts, 1609, which is worth quoting:

> The weaker sexes strongest precedent
> Lyes here belowe seaven fayer years she spent
> In wedlock sage and since that merry age
> Sixty one yeares she lived a widow sage
> Humble as Great as full of Grace as Elde
> A second Anna had she but beheld
> Christ in his Flesh whom now she glorious sees
> Belowe that first in time not in degrees

And round the border: "Anne Butts widowe changed this mortal life for an immortal the 21 of December 1609. She was the daughter and coheir of Henrye Bures Esq. Wife to Edmund Butts Esq. and Mother to the Lady Anne Bacon Wife of Sr. Nicholas Bacon Knight who was her only child."

The following citation from the Consistorial Court of Norwich, to be found in the *East Anglian Notes and Queries*, Volume I, 1864, is of great interest. It is dated 10th October 16II in St Mary's Church, Bury:

"John Purdey keepeth not with his wife: he keepeth at Riborowe in Norfolk." Both were cited to appear on the 25th October, to answer the above presentment, which, neglecting to do, they were excommunicated. Annexed to the pages on which the above presentment occurs is a letter from Lady Anne Bacon, of which the following is a transcript:

Sir — Whereas I do understand that there is a neighbour of mine in Redgrave, the wife of John Purdy, and the daughter of a kinswoman of my husband, who is now excommunicate, as we take it, for that she liveth not with her husband: who although he hath a house and lands in the Town, yet hath his course of life been so unthrifty and ill governed, as it is not known at this day where he is resident, but rather had his abode some time in Norfolk: and other while in Suffolk. I thought it not amiss to inform you truly of the carriage of the woman who hath tasten of much affliction, by his ungodly using of her, as this bearer can truly advertise you; so as by both their consents she was content to take a small allowance from him, and so to live quietly by herself till such time as it please God to give him a better heart and affection unto her, and to be a settled dweller in the Towne: And in the time of her absence, she hath sent him tokens of her love and remembrance of him. And he being visited with sickness this summer, she repaired unto him, and performed the duties of a wife, in keeping and comforting of him. And surely if he be not changed in his life, it is to be feared worse matter may come of their being together than is now. But surely if her cause be truly known and judged aright, it will be found she deserveth small cause of so hard usage. I should be glad if by your favour she might receive some comfort, which I shall take very thankfully and rest ready to requite it with thanks. And thus forbearing further to trouble you I rest
Your friend Anne Bacon.
To my loving friend Mr Robinson, the Registrar of Norwich.

This letter had the desired effect, for there is a memorandum under the presentment of the wife, that she was afterwards absolved gratis, as there was exhibited a letter from the worshipfull Lady Anne Bacon.

This takes us to Nathaniel who had inherited Culford Hall and who sought the hand of the nearby Lady Jane Cornwallis, a very eligible young widow with one son, Frederick Cornwallis. At first she was indignant, thinking he was after her estates and wealth. However, they were married on 1st May 1614 at Brome Church. Their first child, named Anne after Nathaniel's mother, was born in 1615, and a boy, Nicholas, in 1617.

James I visited Culford shortly before the Queen's death, taking with him Prince Charles, later Charles I, when they were staying at Newmarket.

A little touch of life at this period is given in a letter from Nathaniel to his wife, beginning: "Sweet Hart . . . For my health, I cannot wright as I did last, for this week I suffered more payne in my teeth than ever, and this night I slept not one hower, and am now goinge to the mountebank at Bury to draw them out. For ye children, they are in very good health. Nick sends you word of a brood of young chickens, and of a disaster he escaped and my beinge with him, for he eate so much milk porrage at supper that he cryed out, I think I have almost broke myne gutt; and I was fayne to walk him a turne or two about the chamber to digest it."

Nathaniel became a Knight of the Bath in honour of the coronation of Charles I in 1625, and died in 1627. Lady Jane died in 1659 and was buried in Culford church next to her husband.

The next heir, another Nicholas Bacon, who had been imprisoned for debt of £600, died at the early age of forth-three in 1660. He was described as a man of great modesty; he became M.P. for Ipswich and was knighted in 1627. He died without issue and the estate passed to Sir Frederick Cornwallis, who was created Baron Cornwallis of Eye and Treasurer of His Majesty's Household when Charles II came back from exile.

This brings us to the Bacons of Shrubland Hall, which remained in the family for some four generations. The first of the line appears to have been an Edward Bacon, M.P. for Great Yarmouth circa 1575-83, Tavistock 1584-5. Weymouth and Melcombe Regis, 1586-7.

Nathaniel Bacon, his third son, was M.P. for Cambridge University in 1645, till secluded in 1648, and for Ipswich, 1654-6, 1656-8, 1659, and 1660 until his decease. He held several public offices, being appointed Master of requests in 1643, Recorder of Ipswich in 1651, and town clerk in 1652. He was a Bencher of Gray's Inn, Recorder of Bury St Edmunds, Chairman of the Seven Associated Counties, and finally Judge of the Admiralty. The registers of Grays Inn contain many Bacon entries.

The Shrubland Bacons are well represented in the Barham and Coddenham Registers. Taking Barham first, the baptisms amount to fourteen from 1634 to 1638, with a note that the pages of the years 1577 to 1618 are lost. The marriages from 1610 to 1678 numbered only three; burials 1598 to 1688, twenty-two. The Bacon chapel is on the north side of the church.

Turning to the Coddenham registers, baptisms from 1589 to 1732 are twenty-two; marriages six, one of which was that of Philip Bedingfield to Anne Bacon; burials from 1611 to 1795 amount to twenty.

There is a mural tablet in the chancel at Coddenham to Captain Philip Bacon which is of interest to quote:

Here resteth the body of Captain Philip Bacon, second son of Nicholas Bacon of Shrubland Hall, Esquire, on the body of Martha Bingham, the only child of Sir Richard Bingham, Knight of the ancient family of the Binghams of Bigham Melcombe, in the county of Dorset, which said Captain Bacon in the time of King Charles the Second, when his Majestie was in his lowest condition, gat over into Flanders. Soon after by the favour of Sir Charles Berkley; afterwards Lord Fitz-harden, getting into the Duke of York's troupe, to show his new master a little of his bravery . . . he was met by three Frenchmen from whom he received two shot, one in the shoulder and the other in the forehead; the bullet in the forehead had killed him, had it not been for a whipcord hatband, which made it stick, while it was taken out by the Duke himself, the mark of which he brought to this place. Upon this, the Duke taking him in his favour, after the battle of Dunkirk, made him cornet of a troupe of horse, when with his Sacred Soverign and dear Master the Duke, he suffered too many perils and hardships to be here related. Soon after his Majestie's happy restoration, he came into England, and going to volunteer in the first expedition with Sir John Lawson when those honourable Articles were gained with Algiers, he was made Lieutenant to Captain Wye in the Assistance; in the next Expedition to the Straights, he went Lieutenant to Captain Berkely, afterwards Sir William Berkley, in the Bonaventure. In the third expedition to the Straights, when the Second Articles were made with Algiers, he went Lieutenant to Captain Allen, now Sir Thomas Allen, in the St Andrew; at his return, he was made Captain of the Oxford Frigott of 28 guns, with which in the first Dutch battle fought by the Duke of York, for his good service he was made Captain of the Assurance Friggott of 38 guns, with which he fought board by board with the West Freezeland, a Dutch Flagg-ship of 50 guns, while he took her flaggs, which remain in Shrubland Hall at this day; for this he was made Captain of the Bristoll Friggott of 52 guns, and upon his return in her with Sir Jeremy Smith out of the Straights as soon as could possibly careen, and getting out, began that fatal Battle of the

first of June, Anno Dni 1666, in the which he, being the first that
discovered the Dutch Fleet in obedience to Command, he fought
that day with much honour, and the next day until three in the
afternoon, and then came the fatal bullet which took off his thigh,
both the thighs of the Master of the Ship, and the Head of a
common Soldier, by which he honourably ended this transitory life,
to the great lamentation both of King and Duke, and all that knew
him; his ship having very little of her masts and rigging left, soon
after left the fight, bringing his body to Harwich, and the ship when
examined by Captain Deane the King's builder there (beside the loss
of her masts and rigging) had a hundred and eighty shot in her hull,
three of those bullets which were taken out of her, being given by
the said Captain Deane to Sir Nicholas Bacon remain in Shrubland
Hall at this day; his body being brought from Harwich to Ipswich by
water, having all the funeral rites done him by most of the Town,
and a troop of the King's horse; he was conducted through the Town
and from thence to this place, where we must leave him in hopes of
a glorious resurrection.

Surely a most interesting and homely account of a local
amphibious hero.

In 1674 three youthful members of the family are
recorded as scholars at Woodbridge School: Philippus,
Nathaniel and Franciscus Bacon.

It would appear that the line died out about 1796,
according to a tablet on the south wall of the chancel, of
which I quote the relevant portion: "Sacred to the memory
of Nicholas Bacon, M.A. Vicar of Coddenham and Rector of
Barham in this county. Youngest and only surviving son of
Nicholas Bacon, Esquire, descended from the Ancient and
honourable family of Bacon of Redgrave, Suffolk: He
married September 19, 1780, Anna Maria, daughter of John
Brown, Gent. of Ipswich, who died August 9, 1783, by
whom he left no issue. He died after a short illness, August
26, 1796, in the 66th year of his age."

The old hall was pulled down about the date of this old
parson's death. According to an article in *Country Life* for
1900, concerning the present building which was built by Sir
Charles Barry in 1830, some remains of the original house
still existed. The date 1637 and the initials N.B. showed that
it was probably built in the latter days of its tenure by the
Bacons.

The Reverend Edmund Farrer in his *Monumental Brasses* for Suffolk lists several for the Bacon family. First comes that for Sir . . . de Bacon, c. 1320 at Gorleston. This is described as "a mutilated example, in so-called banded mail, cross-legged, and illustrating the gradual addition of plate armour, the armpits, arms and elbows being protected by steel plates covering the mail. The body armour is covered by a surcoat, which is in this case again confined round the waist by a band, and the sword with enriched scabbard is suspended from a bawdrick hanging loosely round the hips; the knee pieces are probably of leather, whilst just enough remains to show that the shins were defended by steel plates. On his left arm is a small heater-shaped shield with the arms of the Bacon family thereon, and suspended by a narrow belt crossing the body diagonally. To his shoulders are attached the ailettes, or little wings, edged with fringe, and each charged with a plain cross, being the last example of the use on brass figures of this curious appendage."

Next comes Sir Adam de Bacon, rector c.1310, at Oulton. An engraving and description of this brass appears in Volume 2 of Suckling's *History of Suffolk*, who writes: "In the centre of the chancel floor lies the full-sized effigy of an ecclesiastic, habited in the gorgeous sacerdotal vestments of the Roman Church . . . Le Neve tells us the figure 'was for Sire Bacon, presbyter, blazoned like those on the shield borne by the Knight of Gorleston.' " Then follows a quotation from a Mr Ives, who considered this skilfully-executed figure to be the oldest sepulchral brass placed to an ecclesiastic now remaining in England; and in spirited design and magnitude, as unsurpassed by any. Unfortunately, this, with other magnificent brasses in this church were stolen in 1857.

There is a brass in Cowlinge church to Ann, daughter of Thomas Dersley, Gent. married to Edward Bacon Esq., of Hessett.

At Petistree there is an effigy of a civilian in long gown, trimmed with fur and two wives in Paris head-dresses, one with a brocaded petticoat. Francis Bacon, 1580. He was the third son of Edmund Bacon of Hessett Esq., and married first, Elizabeth, daughter of . . . Cotton of Barton. By her he had a daughter, Elizabeth. His second wife was Mary, daughter and heir of George Blenerhaysett, Esq., and by her he had no issue.

It might be mentioned here that an Edmund Bacon, son of Edmund Bacon, Esq. born at Hessett, was educated at home under Dr Whitwham and Mr Bridges. Aged 16, he was admitted to Gonville and Caius College, Cambridge, as a fellow commoner, Feb. 22, 159⅜ (sic). At Little Glemham there is a shield and inscription to Sir John Glemham, Knt., 1535. He married a Bacon of Baconsthorpe, and had children.

11

Elizabethan Woodbridge

Here they lived and here they greeted,
Maids and matrons, sons and sires
Wandering in its walks, or seated
Round its hospitable fires.

We might now turn to the very pleasant and picturesque
town of Woodbridge, built as it is on the slope of a hillside
overlooking the Deben, across to the green banks of Sutton,
that holds so much of historic Suffolk in its sandy soil. This
is somewhat removed from the village life of Acton and
Westhorpe, because it was once a port, and a small garrison
town at that. Here also was an Augustinian priory which was
founded in the reign of Henry II, either a little before or a
little after the market in 1161.

It brings us also to Thomas Seckford, Esq., one of the
Masters of the Court of Requests and Surveyor of the Court
of Wards and Liveries, in the reign of Queen Elizabeth. In
other words, a lawyer; and it was he who founded the
almshouses in Woodbridge in 1587, and endowed them by
lands he possessed in Clerkenwell, which as the years passed
made them exceedingly rich.

But he did more than that, because " . . .through whose
Patronage to his Servant Christopher Saxton, we are obliged
for the first maps of the Counties. By the Encouragement
and at the Expence of his Master, Saxton undertook and
published a compleat Set of Maps on the Counties of England
and Wales, many of which he engraved himself, and in the
remainder he was assisted by Remegius Hogenius Hogenbergh
and Others. The County Maps, dedicated to the Queen and
adorned with the Royal arms, and those of the promoter,
Master Sekeford, were published by Saxton in 1579, the
dates on different plates showing that the labour of Six

Years, that is from 1574 to 1579, both included, had been bestowed on them."

There were no less than forty ordinances and statutes governing those pretty little almshouses. "First, — where I have builded seven rooms of brick and stone, with two stories and a garret in every of them [in other words a dormer]. I ordain that in every one of the six of the seven rooms that be westward, two poor persons *unmarried*, shall be placed and set, and in the seventh room or building, at the east end of the said Almes Houses, one poor man *Unmarried*, whom I name and Assign to be one William Marshall, now or late servant to Thomas Brooke esquire . . . which said William Marshall, and every other poor man to be placed in the east-end of the said Almes House. I ordain, to be principal of all the other twelve poor men aforesaid."

They were to have a little garden, in which to grow vegetables, an allotment: a well or 'fountain', and two or three other poor women in other houses nearby, to look after them in case of sickness.

He also ordained that "12 or 13 poor men should have five and twenty shillings paid at the Birth of our Lord, Annunciation of the blessed Virgin, the nativity of St John Baptist and St Michael the Archangel." They were also to have three loads of wood, or in lieu 15s. But the principal was to have 33s. 4d. on the feast days already noted.

All the inmates were to have a gown of two and a half yards of broadcloth, of the price of six shillings a yard, every year between the feast of Sts Michael and All Saints. This was to be adorned by a badge or cognizance of silver, "containing in an estcutcheon the single Coat of our Name and Family, with a sentence written about the same". This was to be worn on the left breast when they attended church or went into the town.

An interesting list of the inmates is given by Loder in his account for 1st January 1792.

Principal		Admitted	Age
William Swaine Sen.	Writing Master	26 Jan. 1788	64
Almsmen			
James Hugging	Peruke Maker	20 Jan. 1784	64
Thomas Peacock	Tailor	17 Oct. 1785	58
Moses Coe	Labourer	6 July 1779	62
William Carlton	Peruke Maker	4 Aug 1787	60
William Norfield	Innholder	13 Nov. 1789	70
Thomas Girling	Grocer	29 Nov 1777	46
Thomas Allison	Carpenter	13 May 1758	69
Thomas List	Labourer	9 Aug 1774	58
Thomas Parish	Bricklayer	5 July 1776	56
Phillip Eade	Carpenter	30 Oct 1789	60
Robert Howell	Innholder	11 March 1785	51
Abraham Church	Peruke Maker	30 Dec 1791	68
Nurses			
Sarah Kell	Widow	25 March 1791	56
Mary Rye	Widow	23 Dec 1782	57
Mary Buttrum	Widow	29 Oct 1789	51

Seckford Hall, which is really in Great Bealings, was built in the reign of Edward II and was in the family until 1673.

This brings us to Woodbridge itself, which has benefited so largely by the Seckford Charities in school, hospital, library and such like. It has been always greatly beloved by its sons and daughters who have had the good luck to be born or to live there.

Richard Garrett, the founder of the famous ironworks at Leiston, was born and educated there in 1766. He was famous for his sickles, then so much in use. His father was a whitesmith and carried on his business in the thoroughfare at the corner of New Street.

Edward FitzGerald was born at Bredfield House. When he lived at Farlingay Hall (which I note has been described as Farthing Cake Hall, because it was built by a baker). He was visited by Tennyson and Carlyle. He took the former to the Bull Hotel, where a remarkable trade in horses was conducted. The covered riding school was a hundred yards long and used for the purpose of training horses. There was stabling for 130 horses, their value ranging from eighty to two hundred guineas. One room at the 'Bull' was like a jeweller's shop, because the trophies won were on show there. But the huge medal pinned on the owner's coat by

Queen Victoria at the Windsor Show was his greatest pride. It was said about 1890 that this business took more people to Woodbridge than any other, and more than one of the crowned heads of Europe had gone there to purchase horses. Tennyson's visit was a disappointment to the owner, because the poet did not know anything about horses and cared less.

Sackcloth was made at Woodbridge in large quantities in the eighteenth century. Fine Woodbridge salt, extracted by the corporation from sea water, was as notable as that produced at Nantwich.

Nonconformity held great sway here, as at other East Coast regions. For example, in 1650 the ringers were paid 6s. for ringing on Thanksgiving Day, 30th January, which was the anniversary of the execution of Charles I. In the *East Anglian Miscellany*, No 11, 670, "The Suffolk Pulpit", there is a note worth quoting:

> Ipswich Wesleyan Methodists. The Rev G. Blanchflower [a lovely name] and G. Rowe. The Rev George Blanchflower, superintendant, a native of Ipswich, appointed after 11 years as a missionary in the West Indies. Very hard upon poor human nature, condemning where he might sympathise and condole . . . During the three years he has resided in Ipswich he has considerably improved as a preacher.
>
> His colleague, the Rev George Stringer Rowe, stationed at Woodbridge, preaches at Ipswich four or five times a month. About 24 years of age, excellent preacher, "though sometimes quaint in expression, he never verges on Spurgeon impudence".

There is an organ in the chapel, so that the opposition to instrumental music among Methodists is not so great, we suppose, as formerly . . . One preacher, the Reverend Philip Garrett, it is said, declared from the pulpit, "That if he saw the Devil running away with that box of whistles [meaning the organ], he would not cry stop thief".

Mrs S. Bedwell (1759-1841) died at Woodbridge. She was formerly housekeeper to Mrs Doughty, and by her penurious habits had acquired considerable property. In a tin canister were found more than seventy soverigns. She possessed money in the bank and held mortages to the value of

£15,000. She had in her possession seventy-five chemises, thirty bonnets, twenty-five silk gowns and four dozen damask tablecloths, and a chest of bed linen; yet she expired covered with merely a piece of old carpet, without a nightcap and in a filthy state. *Ipswich Journal*, 1841.

Woodbridge for many a year had a carrier plying between there and London. In 1625 they bought sixteen leather fire buckets for £2. 0s. 6d. and paid Hayward 1s. 6d. for bringing them home from London. Then in 1658 they bought an eight-hour glass for the use of the sexton, but that does not imply the sermons were that long. In 1664 they were generous enough to give "a sea-broken man" sixpence.

That Woodbridge was connected with great events was once evident in the old priory church, from whence comes the following:

The names of certain persons registered in this monastery in a table, for whose souls the prior and Convent were bound to pray and say Mass.

Sir Hugh Rous, or Red, the Founder, and six other Knights of the same surname. Sir Richard Brews, Knight, lord of Stradbrooke, Patron of the Church with seven other Knights of the same surname, and their wives. Sir Robert de Ufford and Dame Cecily his Wife. Robert de Ufford, Earl of Suffolk, and Dame Margaret his wife.

This Robert, who was also Knight of the Garter, lord of Eye and Framlingham, he and William Montague, Earl of Salisbury, were Generals of King Edward's Army in Flanders, when he went to make his claim to the Crown of France. He served under the Black Prince at the Battle of Poitiers, where John, the French King was taken prisoner. He died at the forty-third year of King Edward III, on the Sunday after All Sants. He was buried in the church of Rendlesham with Cisely his wife.

There was a memorial also to Nathaniel Fairfax, M.D., born 24th July 1637, died 12th June 1690. He was the author of a treatise on the *Bulk and Selvege of the World*. A letter from him is inserted in the third volume of Birch's *History of the Royal Society*. It concerns a young lady who attempted to starve herself, but after ten weeks trial desisted and recovered.

Yet another on the south side of the chancel was to

Philippus Gillet, alias Candler, who died 6th October 1689. (He was descended from an ancient family of that surname which formerly resided at Yoxford. He was Master of the Grammar School here 19 years, which had then the credit of producing a list of Gentlemen of rank and character, who, after receiving their education in that seminary, became the brightest ornaments of this Country.)

Then follows this extract of a will of Mr John Rudland, late of Woodbridge, surgeon, dated 1781.

... my Mind is, that he the said John Ridley, his Heirs or Assigns, shall pay out of my real estate (lying and being in Woodbridge-Hasketon, now in the occupation of Francis Buttrum) so given and devised unto him and them, a clear yearly annuity, or sum of three pounds of lawful money of great Britain without any deduction of taxes, or otherwise, which I will and order, shall be paid on the last day of February, yearly, and every year, for ever, into the hands of the pastor and deacons (for the time being) of the Congregational Meeting House in Woodbridge aforesaid; of which the Rev John Palmer is now pastor; In trust to be laid out by the said pastor and deacons as they in their discretion shall think fit, for three gowns for three poor Widows yearly, on the 2nd day of April, in every year for ever. — And in case default shall be made by the said John Ridley, his heirs or assigns, in payment of the said annuity, or yearly sum of three pounds, as above mentioned, or any part of it, then it shall and may be lawful for the said pastor and deacons, to whom default in payment shall be made, to seize, enter into, and upon the aforesaid estate and premises charged therewith, or into any part thereof, in the name of the whole, and the rents, issues, and profits thereof to receive and take for the use and purpose aforesaid, until the said annuity or such part thereof to receive and take for the use and purpose aforesaid, until the said annuity, or such part thereof as shall be in arrears, shall be fully paid and satisfied, with lawful interest for the same, and all costs and charges occasioned by nonpayment thereof.

12

Medical Matters

He was kind, and loved to sit
In the low hut or garnish'd cottage,
And praise the farmer's homely wit,
And share the widow's homelier pottage:
At his approach complaints grew mild;
And when his hand unbarr'd the shutter,
The clammy lips of fever smiled
The welcome which they could not utter.

In the church chest of Sts Peter and Paul, Felixstowe, is a poster fifteen inches by twelve and a half, exhibiting a fine bit of printing. It is headed with the Hanoverian Arms of England, dated in the year of the Reform Act, 1832, and reads as follows:

By the King, a proclamation for a general fast, William R.

We, taking onto Our most serious consideration the dangers with which this country is threatened by the progress of a grievous disease heretofore unknown in these islands, have resolved, and do by and with the advice of our Privy Council, hereby concerned. That a public day of fasting and humiliation be observed throughout those parts of the United Kingdom called England and Ireland, on Wednesday, the twenty-first day of March next ensuing that so both we and our people may humble ourselves before Almighty God, in order to obtain pardon of our sins, and in the most devout and solemn manner send up our prayers and supplications to the divine majesty, for averting these heavy judgements which our manifold provocations have most justly deserved; and particularly beseeching God to remove us from that grievous disease with which several places in the Kingdom are at this time visited. And we do strictly charge and command the said public fast be reverently and devoutly observed by all our living subjects in England and Ireland as they tender the favour of Almighty God, and would avoid his wrath and indignation; and upon pain of such punishment as may be justly inflicted on all such as continue and neglect the performance of so religious and necessary a duty. And for the better and more orderly solemnising the same, we have given directions to the Most Reverend the Archbishops and the Right Reverned the Bishops of England and Ireland to compose a form of prayer suitable to this occasion, to be used in all churches, chapels and places of public worship, and to take care that the same be timely dispersed through their respective dioceses.

Given at our court at Saint James's this Six Day of February One thousand eight hundred and thirty two, in the Second Year of Our Reign.

God save the King.

I wonder if this was duly observed in the then small village of Felixstowe and its tiny church? If so, this bill shows no sign of having been exhibited. It is addressed on the back to the officiating minister, Walton, under which Felixstowe was then a curacy.

England was then, and for many years to come, subject to these outbreaks of disease which came into the country through its ports, as also from lack of sanitation. It evidently struck this little spot because five members of the Dickens family died within a few months of one another and are buried there according to a memorial in the church. What was it? Cholera, typhoid, plague, or smallpox might all have been brought in through the port of Harwich or Ipswich. This time it was cholera.

In the first volume of the *Proceedings of the Bury and West Suffolk Archaeological Institute*, Samuel Tymms contributed a paper on "Notes Towards a Medical History of Bury", which he had read on 8th June 1848. This contains some most interesting information. He commences with the note that the science of medicine was first professed by monks and clerks in orders, and that Baldwin, the builder of the magnificent abbey church, had, previous to his election as Abbot of Bury, acted as physician to Edward the Confessor.

Another eminent practitioner there was Walter the Physician, who is mentioned by Jocelin de Brakelond as contributing "much of what he had acquired by his practice of physic" to the erection in 1198 of the new stone almonry, or guest-room for indigent strangers. Leprosy was then a great scourge and the hospital of St Peter without Risby gate was founded for the maintenace of leprous priests, and the hospital of St Petronella, or St Parnell, without the South gate, for leprous maidens. The disease was then considered incurable.

The monks of Bury were well cared for in time of sickness. An infirmarer, or Curator of the Infirmary, was an established officer; a large stone building of many apartments "fitted up with every convenience", was built in 1150 by Hugo the Sacrist, "below the churchyard".

One of the chief sanitary regulations of the house was a periodic blood letting, and this often occasioned confidential talk amongst the brethren. This is what Jocelin had to say about it:

I observed Sampson the Sub-sacrist [afterwards the famous Abbot], as he was sitting along with others (since at all these private assemblies at blood-letting season, the cloister monks were wont mutually to reveal to each other the secrets of their hearts, and to talk over matters with everyone). I saw him, I say, sitting along with others, quietly chuckling, and noting the words of each, and after a lapse of twenty years calling to mind some of the before written opinions . . . Upon one particular occasion I was unable to restrain myself, but must needs blurt out my own private opinions, thinking that I spoke to trusting ears . . . And behold one of the sons of Belial disclosed my saying to a friend and benefactor; for which reason, even to this day, never could I since . . . regain his good will.

This operation was, of course, practised by the barbers and a portion of the Abbeygate Street was formerly known as Barbers' Row. However, poor folk could not afford their charges, neither were there enough barbers to go round, so they had recourse to the "sow-gelders, horse gelders, tinkers and cobblers".

In the accounts for 1575 occur these two entries: "XXVIsVIIJd paid to John Bearham for the healing of a pore diseased wench. XIIJs IIIJd to Liechefilde for the healing of Clayden's legge. "Lichfield it appears was a professional man; for in 1581 is this entry "XLs to Lichfild surgeon for curing a pore man grievously skalt with hot water."

In the following year a travelling female practitioner divided the emoluments as well as the honour: there was bestowed "XLIXs upon a woman surgeon of Colchester and Lychfilde for curing of the wife of John Willye of Bury, and divers others."

1584 LVJs VIIJd bestowed in chirurgery for the curing of Tosse and his wife of . . . Willis infected with the French pocke.

1596 Xs to Atkin for setting of Godfreis legge which was broken.

1597 XXs to old Wretham for cures of certain poor diseased persons.

1606 IJs to Dickenson's wife for taking in hand of a poor woman to heal her of a fistula.

1614 Xs to Ambrose Lichfeild for healing of a poor woman's leg sore hurt with a boar.

IIIJs given to Johnson a poor man in relief that went to the bath [the city of Bath].

1618 To Oliver Tebold for healing Butteries daughter of the falling sickness [epilepsy].

The years 1348-9 were those of the Great Scourage, known as the Black Death, which swept across England, but nowhere more violently than in East Anglia. In the diocese of Norwich it is calculated that two thousand of its clergy perished. The people died by scores, dying where they fell, the man at his plough, the maid at her milking, unattended by family or neighbour, unshriven and uncomforted. The clergy died or fled from their posts.

Bury suffered severely from this disease in 1257, when a thousand persons died of it. Again in 1557 there were many deaths and from August 1578 to March 1579-80, 164 persons are entered in St Mary's register alone. In 1587, the plague came again, when those infected were removed to tents erected in the fields around the town. Then in 1665, in anticipation, the corporation on the 10th August directed "the greate Barne, called Almoner's Barne, to be provided as a pest house."

Smallpox was a frequent visitor. In 1677, according to Gillingwater, it was so prevalent that people resorting to the market by the Risbygate road were accustomed to dip their money in water (tradition said vinegar) which had been placed in the cavity of the ruined base of the boundary cross, situated at the bottom of Chalk Lane. (This was also done at the boundary cross on Barnham Common when the plague raged at Thetford.)

Amongst the list of doctors are several of note. Richard Child commenced his professional career in this town. Of Emmanuel College, Cambridge, he took his M.D. in 1650. In 1656, as appears from the corporation minutes, he "did by a friend freely offer to the Corporation to give his advice to the poor sick people within the burghe, not expecting any fee or reward for the same, which free and charitible offer was very kindly accepted by the Corporation, and therefore ordered that thanks be given to the said Doctor for his said free and christian offer."

Dr Poley Clopton, M.D. 1705, was a resident practitioner. He was the second son of William Clopton of Liston Hall, Essex, and Elizabeth, daughter of Sir William Poley of Boxted. He died on 31st October 1730 aged fifty-six and left the greater part of his estate for the founding of an asylum in the town which bore his name.

John Kerrich, M.B. 1717, M.D. 1722, was a native of Norfolk, educated at Caius College Cambridge but practised in Bury all his professional career, taking over the practice of Dr Hartley. He died 9th October 1765 aged seventy, and a highly eulogistic epitaph was placed in St Mary's by his widow: "He was never at ease himself whilst his patient was in pain or danger; nor found any diminution of his fellow feeling in the misery of others from a long acquaintance by his practice with sickness or suffering. The profession of physic was in his hands a general fund of charity for the indigent, for he chose to make it subservient to the acquisition of treasures in heaven rather than upon earth." She could hardly have said more.

Misael Remon Malfalqueyrat, M.B, a native of France,

carried on an extensive practice in midwifery. He was supposed to have brought more children into the world than any person then living. He died 20th November 1789 aged eighty-seven; seventy of these years had been spent in this town.

There was also a monument to a midwife who had assisted at the birth of 4,323 living children; and another to a Mary Martin, who, according to the register of St Mary's, by her office brought into the world 2,237 children.

There was also Richard Child, M.D. His son, another Richard, became Rector of Groton, and his son (grandson of the first Richard), also named Richard, became a physician, taking his M.B. in 1708 and an M.D. in 1720. He practised in Lavenham, dying in 1766.

But the most remarkable was William Hyde Woolaston, M.B. 1788, M.D. 1793, F.R.C.P. 1795, F.R.S. 1793. He began his medical practice in Huntingdon in 1789, but moved to Bury soon after. He was the third son of the Reverend Francis Woolaston, F.R.S., Rector of Chislehurst, Kent. He practised for some years in Bury before quitting medicine on his removal to London to devote himself to science. He discovered the malleability of platinum.

When at Bury he knew the habitat of every rare plant. When out riding with a friend he suddenly pulled up and exclaimed, "There's the *Linum radiola*", a plant well known but so minute as to escape detection. In a letter to H.E. Bunbury he asked for specimens of rare plants to be sent to him, particularly those to be found about Mildenhall.

Soon after he came to Bury he was called to attend what was thought to be a serious case and asked to give an opinion on it. He replied, "You must consider I am a young man. I see nothing to be alarmed about, but you cannot expect me to speak at once decidedly." He then burst into tears. His acute sympathy with suffering led to his giving up the medical profession. An article devoted to his memory is in the same volume of *Proceedings* by the

Reverend H. Hasted who was rector of Horringer from 1814 to 1852.

Charlton Wollaston, the Doctor Wollaston involved in the Wattisham affair (see below), was the uncle of William Hyde. He practised in Bury for a few years only. Returning to London in 1762 he became physcian to the Queen's household, but unfortunately died of fever in 1764 aged thirty-one.

Also in the *Proceedings* is an article by A.G. Hollingsworth on the "Medical Archaeology of Suffolk." He was the historian of Stowmarket. After a general survey which does not concern the county as such, we get some local information, such as the provision made for leprosy in the lazar hospitals of Ipswich, Bury and Eye. He was evidently unaware of the one at Dunwich.

In 1569 Stowupland paid Mother Swift for the healing of "J. Byrde her legge 10 shillings." He states that "legs male and female appear in the accounts for more than 250 years." A "Mr Guttridge, for setting Ennifer's boye's arms 10s." This seems to have been a fixed sum for both arms and legs at this time of 1645.

The price for bleeding was 6d., and making a seat in the neck 2s. In the *Antiquities of Hengrave* by John Gage, 1822 we are told that when Sir Thomas Kitson died in 1540 and an inventory was taken, amongst the "Wares in the warehouses in London" appeared the curious item: "a hundryth wyght of amletts for the neke . . . 30/4d." Gage then follows with a quotation from Dr Hering's *Preservatives against the Pestilence*: "Perceiving many in this citie to weare about their necks upon the region of the heart certain placents or amulents (as preservatives against the pestilence) confected of arsenick, my opinion is, that they are so farre from effecting any good in this kind, as a preventive, that they are very dangerous and hurtful, if not pernitious to those that weare them."

Returning to Hollingsworth, in 1670, Dr Goodall was paid £2 to attend all the parish poor in Stowmarket. Then in 1690 came the dreadful scourge of smallpox and again in 1748. Midwifery was then managed by women at 2s. 6d. a case.

They were a bit more generous at Hengrave in 1573.

To Dr Attesloe for his paines in coming to my mistress being sicke of the measles, Xs.

To Doctor Langeton for ministering of certayne fysicke unto my master and my mistress at one time XLI VJs.

To the poticary for certain poticary stuffe for my master and my mistress LIXs Xd.

To Mr Barwicke for ministering of fisicke to Mistress Mary Cornwallies, Xs.

Unfortunately for the sick this practice of bleeding was adhered to until well on into the nineteenth century, and the so-called doctor thus accelerated the end of the patient. Even the Duke of Kent, father of Queen Victoria, was bled to death by his doctors. They seemed to work on the old adage that 'soft surgery makes foule sores'. It was even done to sheep at one corner of the eye, sometimes at the upper part of the tail and sometimes the ear. Master, servants, horses and hounds were all bled at intervals.

A rare drink for the scurvy consisted of a draught of watercress, scurvy grass, sage, wormwood, celandine, scabious leaves, agrimony, roots of bitterweed, fennel and parsley. A plaster compounded of all heal and hogs suet was used; and a remedy for rheumatism consisted of a sheet dipped in specially prepared warm lime and water, wrapped round the sufferer.

To which might be added the true hemlock (*Conium maculatum*) which was looked upon as an infallible remedy for sore eyes. But the method of application was remarkable. The leaves of the plant were chopped up fine, white of eggs, baysalt and red ochre were added and the mixture was then applied as a poultice to the left wrist if the right eye was affected and vice versa.

In the little village of Wattisham, the church of which is dismissed in three lines by Munro Cautley, is a most remarkable tablet in the N.W. corner. It reads: "This inscription Serves to Authenticate the Truth of a Singular Calamity, Which Suddenly happened to a poor Family in this Parish, Of which Six Persons lost their Feet by a Mortification not to be accounted for. A Full Narrative of their Case is Recorded in the Parish Register & Philos: Transactions for 1762."

The story concerned John Downing, a poor labourer in the village, his wife Mary and their six children, who were in health until January 1762. On Sunday 10th January the eldest daughter Mary, aged fifteen complained of severe pain in the left leg, particularly in the calf. By nightfall the pain had become excrutiating; she likened it to being gnawed by dogs. The same evening another daughter also suffered from similar pain and by the next day the mother and another child were also in pain. By Tuesday the whole family except the father and the baby had similar symptoms, some in one leg and some in both. The pains continued for several days, then the diseased limbs developed blue spots as though they had been bruised and the affected parts gradually turned black and gangrenous. The flesh sloughed off the bone and in most cases the surgeon simply cut through the dry bone. The eldest girl lost one leg below the knee, but by April the gangrene in the other leg had spread to involve the ham, with a large abcess beneath it; although the surgeon removed the abscess she died. Mrs Downing, aged forty, lost both legs but recovered. Robert, aged eight, lost both legs below the knees, while Edward, aged four, only lost his feet. The father was only slightly affected; the baby died.

This attracted widespread attention. It was reported to the Royal Society by Dr Wollaston and by the minister, the Reverend James Bones. A short report appeared in the *Ipswich Journal* for 17th April and a fuller account on 8th May based on information supplied by Dr Wollaston.

Naturally enough, it was put down to witchcraft by the villagers, but it was agreed by the faculty that it was a case of ergot poisoning caused by contaminated food, probably bread made from poor wheat, but not rye bread as generally reported. It was discovered that the family drank water from a pond, and brewed their own beer, using a big brass kettle. They had lived on pickled pork, pease, milk, cheese and bread. In the period before Christmas 1761 they had eaten ewe mutton.

Doctor David van Zwanenberg has written a monograph on this extra-ordinary outbreak, on which this account is based. He points out that if this was the only instance of gangrenous ergotism due to damaged grain that has been recorded in England, then the person who wrote the inscription in the church used a particularly apt expression when he called it "a singular calamity". Dr Wollaston's letter to the Royal Society was the only publication he wrote concerning Suffolk, where he practised for four years.

Coming to more recent times, we meet Charles Wilson, M.D., member of the Royal Medical Society of Edinburgh and graduate of that University, who lived and practised in Yoxford. In 1815 he published *Observations on Gout And Rheumatism, including An Account Of A Speedy, Safe and Effectual Remedy for those Diseases: with Numerous Cases and Communications.*

He achieved some fame by the success of his tincture and alternative aperient pills, which were administered to the Prince Regent with good effect, although Wilson refused to disclose the ingredients when politely asked to by Lord Henniker on behalf of H.R.H. It is quite obvious the doctor had his eye on the main chance, with a view to a pension or an honour. It is said that George IV presented him with a carriage and pair as a token of his appreciation.

Wilson's desk was still in use in the surgery at Yoxford until a few years ago. Under some of the small drawers were inscriptions made by various of his apprentices, who marked the commencement of their careers but failed to note the dates of their departures.

The *Gout Case Book* is of considerable interest because of its local flavour; while the appendix contains testimonials of a fulsome order, all of which could hardly be described as unsolicited. I append a few of the more inspiring: From Sir Patrick Blake, Bury St Edmunds: ". . . although I have endured the torments of this Proteus-like complaint in both hands and both feet, yet one hand was frightfully bad, as bad as can well be conceived: and the next day, or the day after, one foot and one ankle were fully as bad as the hand, the inflammation being excessive, such as to be termed fine and wholesome gout by the cognoscenti. But after treatment this. Sleep succeeded slumber, and slumber sleep during the whole night, and part of the following day, till about twelve o'clock: and what with sleep, perspiration, and a wonderful relaxation from insufferable pain my thoughts, partly incoherent, seemed to carry me to heaven."

This, from a clergyman who evidently acted as a lay doctor to his gouty parishioners judging from the volume of his correspondence: "Bath, May 1816 . . . I now beg to inform you that I have passed (as usual) through a long winter of repeated gout attacks, all and each of which have been met by your medicine, and gloriously driven from the field." And again: "May the world one day or other, look forward to the knowing of the component parts of the Tincture." And yet further: "Long before midsummer last, a young farmer came to me in Bath to say, that my congregation was in most unworthy hands. We all reached home next day. I had got the Curate out of the house before. Still he bade me defiance, as he was licenced to the curacy: but to obviate this, I gave notice to the Chancellor of the diocese, that I should perform the church duties myself. To the astonishment of myself and others. I got on tolerably well. The people all know that I am a cripple, and perhaps they know also that after being twenty years their Vicar, I do not preach one doctrine and practise another."

And this from a chemist at Bath: "April 1818. I am

visited daily by one or more podagrics, eager to learn what has been my experience of your remedy."

W.A. Maddocks Esq., M.P., writes from Albemarle Street, London, 31st January 1817: "Sir ... Give me leave to ask if you have determined on any means of preserving the purity of your tincture in case any unfortunate accident were to happen to you. It has proved so efficacious in several instances which I know, that I feel anxious for mankind so valuable a secret should not be lost."

T. Wales Esq., surgeon: Downham, Norfolk, 1817, distinguishes between the gout of the well-to-do and the rheumatism of the others: "Since I had the pleasure of seeing you, my son has had several opportunities of trying the effect of your Tincture, in cases of acute rheumatism chiefly among the lower orders."

Captain Baird of the 3rd Regiment of Guards, writes concerning his father: "He wished me, however, to state his case fully to you, namely, the gout which he has by hereditary right, all his ancestors having been very subject to it."

And this as a tailpiece from Col. Sturt, 69th Regiment of Foot, 1813: "Yet the gout and the rheumatism frequently attacks seven or ten joints at a time. I have been powerfully assailed in seventeen distinct unconnected joints at one time, and, without exaggeration, imagine that these several parts kept time in agony as ringing round the peals."

William Henry Williams, M.D. was the inventor of the 'Williams' Field Tournaquet', adopted by the Army Medical Board. He settled down in Ipswich in 1801. Amongst his publications was: *Observations on Dr Wilson's Tincture, the Eau Medicinale, and other pretended Specifics for Gout*, 1818.

It appears that Dr Wilson's second wife, who survived him, kept up the sale of the tincture until 1891, but would not disclose the recipe.

A doctor at Norwich had a novel way with the

extraction of teeth, so much so that he could extract his own. He would fasten a strong piece of catgut round the tooth, to the end of which he fixed a bullet. The bullet was fired from a pistol. When the trigger was pulled out came the tooth without any trouble.

The doctor could but rarely prevail⁻ on his friends to avail themselves of this remedy. Once a gentleman agreed to try the method and had allowed the apparatus to be adjusted, but at the last moment exclaimed, 'Stop, stop, I've changed my mind!" "But I haven't, and you're a fool and a coward for your pains," answered the doctor, pulling the trigger. In another instant the tooth was extracted, much to the patient's delight and astonishment.

Many of the doctors had physick gardens, one of which was at Ipswich. It came to be called Coyte's Garden, although it was started by a William Beeston, (1672-1732). He was the son of the Rector of Sproughton. Another Cambridge man, he graduated in M.B. 1692, M.D. in 1702. He established the garden prior to 1724 when it was visited by Daniel Defoe. He left a lengthy and explicit will in which he entailed the property to his nephew and his nephew's male descendants.

The next owner was his nephew, William Coyte (1708-75), who was born in Woodbridge, went to Ipswich School, and took his M.B. at Cambridge in 1732. He practised medicine in Ipswich and was a botanist of some note. Both he and his uncle Beeston are buried under the aisle of Bentley church.

His son, William Beeston Coyte, 1740-1810 inherited the garden. He became a renowned botanist and a member of the Linnaean Society and published two books: *Hortus Botanicus Gippovicensis* in 1796, *Index Plantarum* in 1807. He died in March 1810 and the garden passed to his younger brother, who was Curate of St Nicholas Church, Ipswich. Some time during the next twenty years the property was sold for house development. The garden is clearly marked on Pennington's Map. There is still a small lane named after Coyte, running into Queen Street.

Some of the more studious of the squirearchy made lists of plants and flowers that grew locally. Here is one made by Sir Thomas Gage, fellow of the Linnaean Society, to be found at Hengrave at the end of the eighteenth century: "Upright wood reed, found in the Hyde Wood. Small teasel in the Bath House Grove. Marsh Violet, in ditches near the river Lark. Blue Pimpernel, Grange Farm. Dark Mullein, Stanchill's Farm. Vineleaved Dropwort, in ponds. Pale Daffodil, in meadows. Deadly Nightshade, in hedgerows. Flowering Rush, Reed pond. Pale Briar in hedgerows. Downy Rose, near Hyde Wood. Silver Cinquefoil, Mill. Mongrel Poppy, Stanchill's Farm. Woolly Snapdragon, in corn fields. Bitter Cress in turnip fields. Purple Milk Vetch, near the Warren hill Pinn. Birds Nest Ophyrys, Hyde Wood. Panicled Sedge, Bath House Cover. Whorled Mill-flower, Reed Pond. Bitter Purple Willow, Grange Farm, Frogbit, Mill ditches. Adder's Tongue, Lime Close."

Now follows the collection made by the Reverend Sir John Cullum at Hawstead:

In corn, Little Field Madder, Thorough Wax, Night-flowering Catch-fly, Wild Larkspur, Pansies or Heart's Ease.

In shady places, Woodroof, Morel (Phallus esculentus); and shady hedges, Hart's Tongue, Male and female Polypody.

By Roadsides, Cromwell, Sage-leaved black Mullen, Wild Succory; and Moneywort in moist places.

In hedges, The greater Periwinkle, Deadly Nightshade, Great Throatwort, Bastard Stone Parsley, Agrimony, Common Columbine, Ploughman's Spikenard, Crosswort or Mugweed, Yellow Nettle hemp, Wild and Small Wild Teasel.

In pastures, Autumnal Gentian, Earth Nut, Purging Flax, Mousetail, Yellow Centaury, White Sengreen, Orpine or Live Long, Crested Cow-Wheat, Dwarf Carline Thistle, Bee Orchis, Burnet, Adder's Tongue.

In Wood, Sanicle, Wild Angelica, Great Burnet Saxifrage, Great Bastard Hellebore, Rough Horse-tail or Shave Grass, Wood Sorrel, Bugle.

In Meadows, Chequered Daffodil or Fritillary, Meadow Saffron, Water Hemlock, Green Man Orchis on dry grassy banks, White

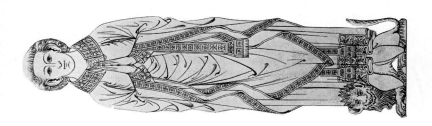

(*left*) Sire Adam Bacon's brass in Oulton Church; (*right*) the font in Cratfield Church (from Suckling's *History of Suffolk*)

A page from a fourteenth-century Book of Hours associated with
Alice de Reydon

Maiden-hair on the church and old walls about the Place; together with Crimson Cup Peziza on half-rotten sticks in shady hedges.

He also gives a very interesting little table concerning the vagaries of spring during the space of five years:

	1779	1784	Diff. in days
Apricot Tree	20 Feb.	15 April	54
Wood Anemone	9 March	16 April	38
Apple tree	6 April	15 May	39
White Thorn	15 April	22 May	37
Vine	14 June	23 June	9
Lime tree	21 June	7 July	16

Sir John then gives us an illuminating and pleasant picture about the health of his "Sweet Auburn":

The air, it should seem, is salubrious, there being no marshes nor stagnating water to load it with noxious vapours. Nor are the inhabitants subject to any particular maladies. They are remarkably free from coughs: and while the places of worship in the metropolis resound with the labouring lungs of the audiences, in this church — "No coughing drowns the parson's saw." Why they are free from this disorder, no better reason can perhaps be given, than that they take no pains to guard against it. Even in winter, one of the church doors often stands open during the whole service, no one thinking it worth while to rise and shut it. Yet for some reason or other this place is not so favourable to Human life as some others, about 1 in 47 dying annually these last 14 years. But it is to adults that it seems less friendly; for to infant life it is very propitious. In these last 14 years, 188 children have been christened here; during which time only 36 have died under two years of age, which is about 1 in 6. The most prolific year in that period was 1775, which produced 22 children; not one of which died under two years of age. In great cities, I believe about one third that are born are swept away under that age. The most fatal period here seems the first year.

> She little promis'd much,
> Too soon untide;
> She only dreamt she liv'd,
> And then she dyde.

13

Extracts from FitzGerald's Sea Words and Phrases

They have been at a great feat of languages, and stolen the scraps.
O! they have lived long on the alms basket of words. I marvel thy
master hath not eaten thee for a word; for thou art not so long by
the head as honorificabilitudinitatibus: thou art easier swallowed
than a flap-dragon.

Edward FitzGerald in 1865 contributed a collection of sea
words and phrases to the *East Anglian*. Some of these had
appeared in other vocabularies, but generally they were
current phraseology along the Suffolk coast. I give the
concluding paragraph of his introduction:

Meanwhile, you think these words of mine may find a proper
niche in your East Anglian; and you are very welcome to them.
Picked up idly, with little care how or whence they came to hand,
I doubt they will make a sorry show in your grave pages, whether
as regards quantity or quality. They may, however, amuse some of
your readers, and perhaps interest others in guessing at their history.
On the whole, I think if you print them, it must be in some
Christmas number, a season when even antiquaries grow young,
scholars unbend, and grave men are content to let others trifle.
Even *Notes and Queries*, with all the scholars that Bruce so long
has led, sometimes smile, sometimes doze, and usually gossip
about what is now the fashion to call Folk-lore at Christmas. And
so, wishing you at any rate, a happy one, I remain, your's very
sincerely, E.F.G.

Undoubtedly these words had been in use for centuries,
but it is the phrases that are so good, with a true old
Suffolk ring.

Armstrong. arm in arm: "they came hallorin' down the street
armstrong." A good word surely.

Bark. "The surf *bark* from the Nor'ard;" or, as was otherwise said to me, "the sea aint lost his woice from the Nor'ard yet," a sign by the way, that the wind is to come from that quarter.

A poetical word, such as those whose business is with the sea are apt to use. Listening one night to the sea some way inland, a sailor said to me, "Yes, sir, the sea roar for the loss of the wind; "which a landsman properly interpreted as only meaning that the sea made itself heard when the wind had subsided.

Barm-skin. The oil skin, or "oily" which covers the fisherman's *barm* or bosom, and reaches to the *petticoats* of the same material, covering the lower man.

Bean. "To throw in a bean" — to put in one's oar-throw in an objection; or as I once heard an old fashioned Farm-wife say to her husband — "Joe, bor, you must hull in an Obistacle." She was speaking of an ill-devised marriage of her son's.

Beggar's Opera. A hostelry for tramps, &c.

Betty. To be over nice in putting things in order. "He go betty, betty, bettyin' about the boat like an old woman."

Black Meat. Cured bacon.

Blare. A mixture of pitch and tar.

Blowfish. Often met with by North-sea herring men; they tell me it is the whale. (Query?)

Bottom's Out. The bottom of the sea, when beyond reach of the lead.

Bows. Prounced as rose, But query (bowse?) beer.

So at least is the following inventory, which I am told comprises a fair fisherman's breakfast "a pint of bows, a penny buster (*sc.* burster, a penny loaf), a bit of kessen (cheese), a stinger (onion), and a pinch of tomtartarum (salt)."

Breach. I have heard this form of *break* used with force. "There she lie, the sea breachin' over her."

Brenner. A sharp gust of wind on the water.

Brouge. To scorch? Men and boats "broughin' about in a hot calm."

Brustle. A compound of *Bustle* and *Rustle*, I suppose. "Why, the old gril brustle along like a Hedge-sparrow!" said of a round-bowed vessel spuffling through the water.

I am told that, comparing little with great, the figure is not out of the way. Otherwise what should these ignorant seamen know of Hedge-sparrows? Some of them do, however; fond of birds as of other pets — Children, cats and dogs — anything in short consider-ably under the size of — a Bullock — and accustomed to birds-nesting over your cliff and about your lanes from childhood. A little while ago a party of Beachmen must needs have a day's frolic at the old sport; marched boldly into a neighbouring farmer's domain, ransacked the hedges, climbed the trees, coming down pretty figures I was told (in plainer language) with guernsey and breeches torn fore and aft; the farmer after them in a tearing rage, calling for his gun – "They were Pirates! – They were the Press-gang!" and the boys in blue going on with their game laughing. When they had got their fill of it, they adjourned to Oulton Boar for "Half a Pint"; by and by in came the raging farmer for a like purpose; at first growling aloof; they warming toward the good fellows, till – he joined their company, and – insisted on paying their shot!

Brot-tow. (As I suppose from the derivation suggested to me, viz., A.S. *gebrotu*, fragments; but sounded *Braw-toe*) scraps and fragments of rope collected to make coarse paper of.

An old fellow –an old Waterloo fellow too – used to go by the name of "Old Brawtoe" among the beachmen, because of his dealing in this line.

Bull. "He know no more of Herrin'-drivin' than a Bull does of Sunday." And again, "He spuffled about till he 'sweat like a Bull.' "

Burn. "How the sea burn!" What you now hear children talk of as "being in a state of phosphorescence." Which is best?

Butterfly. Considered lucky, and therefore tenderly entreated, when straying into house, or net-chamber. I am told by a learned Professor that the same belief prevails in India.

Caravan-hat. The old-fashioned Poke-bonnet; or the present fashion "produced" by the modern "Ugly"; like the tilt of a covered cart.

Candle out of Binnacle. "He soon ran the candle out o' the "Binnacle;" *sc.* all the money out of his pocket.

Chuckle. Clumsy, coarse. Among all the fishes of the sea that rise out of the deep to warn the seaman of foul weather – "Up come the cod-fish with his chuckle head."

Clock-Calm. "The sea was all clock-calm."

Calm as one of our venerable old-fashioned eight-day clocks, with its open countenance and steady pulsation. The phrase will die away with them, for the new American timepieces don't hold up the same mirror to nature.

Coach; Coached. Out of pocket. "I', coach'd," or "I'm Coach."

Chopp'd Hay. Smuggled tobacco.

Cock's-Eye. A bright opening in a dark sky.

A bright thought of some Southwold sailor perhaps, for I was told at Lowestoft that "the Southwold men were great men for the Cock's-eye.

Company Keepers. Ships that sail together, as well as Lovers who "walk" together. "That old Jemima and Wiolet (Violet) are rare company keepers."

Complain. A ship or boat begins to *complain* when her nails, seams, or timbers, begin to give way.

Core or Coar. To untwist a rope or line from its *kinks.*

Dan or Den. A small buoy, with some ensign atop, to mark where the fishing lines have been *shot*; and the *dan* is said to "watch well" if it hold erect against wind and tide.

Dart. "Dart before the wind," the wind right aft; or, as I once heard a foreigner say, "in *my behind.*"

"Deep as the North-star;" said (by a conger-eel man) of a very *wide-a-wake* babe, four months old.

Dollar. "Shine like a Dollar"; said by a Sailor of a Pony that he got up after her holiday in the marshes-duly holding a bit of bread to windward, he told me — and her coat was "as fine as a star," he said, "shine like a Dollar, that ta did."

Domino. Unoccupied. "The house lay domino this twelve-month."

Drabble-tail. Draggle-tail; a vessel so lean aft as to "slap her starn" into the seas; also called a "slap-tailer." Two Guernseys colloguing over a half-pint; A., "You know, Duffer" (B's *nom de mer*) "that old Jemima of yours is a regular Drabble-tail." B. (who has hitherto vindicated his ship as best of the bunch), "Hang her, she's an old-witch. Let's have another half pint."

Drope. Downward inclination.

Fag Out, Fray out as a rope's end. So the "fag end" of anything.

Fair. Clouds running to. "Do you think the wind 'll hold?" "Lord bless ye, look at the clouds a runnin' to a fair like."

Fake. A Take or Catch. I suppose from Danish.

Fanny About. A light variable wind fannies about.

Feather-white. "The sea was all a "feather-white" with foam.

Fiddle. "Kept her like a fiddle."

This little piece of wood and catgut, to draw forth whose wonderful speech seemed to Johnson the greatest wonder of human handicraft has, we know, always had its charm for the sailor, whether on duty at sea, or *not* on duty ashore. Who can resist the delightful saucy "sailors' hornpike," step or music? I really think the only national dance we have. So the sailor has taken the fiddle to compare the craft he loves to. "Kept her like a fiddle;" he says of one who takes care of his craft; "she goes like a wiolin," of the smart vessel herself, swift and glib as "the melody that's sweetly play'd in tune. "And, by the way, I have heard them talk of "givin' her a tunin' " — *sc.* by trying her, her spars, and rigging, in such a sea and wind, that if she weather all that, she may be relied upon in any case.

Fine Weather Flop. An unexpected dash of water over a vessel's sides in fine weather, and on a smooth sea.

Flad Sky. Fled sky? Cloud that has settled in a bank to leeward.

Folt. To lap up a wet sail loosely, so as air may get in; *not* the same as *fold*, I hear; perhaps a looser form of it.

Foot Loose. A vessel so disengaged from dock that she can start whenever she pleases. A pretty word.

Frothy. Too light on the water (a vessel), as from insufficient ballast: such I heard said, "Come a breeze, the old girl would blow away like a thistle blossom."

Friday. By some a change of weather — even from bad to better — is look'd for on a Friday. I have often laughed at this, and — found it right.

Gast-cope. (I know not how else to write it, nor how at all to account for it), "Going gast-cope, "without hire or pay, as a boy on his first trial voyage.

Gin. "Clear as gin." A sailor's best compliment to water.

Gowry. Greedy, voracious.

Hank. Stoppage. "Come to a dead hank," as by a change of wind, a calm, &c. Query *hang?*

Herrin'-spink. (I thought "Heron spink") the Golden crested Wren, often caught by the hand while "latching" in the rigging, or among the gear, during the North Sea Fishing.

These little birds, it seems, are then crossing the seas for the winter, and have been found, I am told, cluster'd almost like bees along the hedges near Caistor: so tired as to be taken by hand on shore, as by the sailors at sea. I find they call the bird "Woodcock Pilot" further north; being supposed to herald the Woodcock two days in advance.

Holiday. Any interval which the tarrer or varnisher of a vessel has neglected to cover. "Jem have left plenty of holidays, anyhow."

Horrywaur. Fifty pounds to the philologer who will guess this riddle without looking to the end for its solution.

When first I knew Lowestoft, some forty years ago, the herring luggers (which then lay up on the beach, when not at sea), very many of them bore testimony to Wesley's visits to the place, and his influence on the people. Besides the family and familiar names, such as the William, Sarah Jane, Two Friends, Brothers, and such like; there were the Ebenezer, Barzillai, Salem, and many more

Old Testament names; beside the Faith, Hope, Charity, &c from later Revelation. A few vessels bore names in profane story — such as Shannon (which, by the way, still reigns) after Sir Philip Broke's victory; there was even William Tell (no longer reigning), whose effigies, drest in an English sailor's white ducks and blue jackets, pointed at the wind with a pistol at the mast-head. That was about the furthest reach of legendary or historical lore. But now the schoolmaster has been at sea, as well as abroad, and gone herring-driving — Bless me! ther's now a "Nil Desperandum," a "Dum Spiro Spero," and last, not least, a Meum and Teum; "though in the latter case it was very properly represented to the owners that the phrase being in Latin, should properly run "Meum et Tuum." Then even the detested *Parley-vous* has come into request; and you may hear of a Scrunk of luggers very gravely enumerated in such order as the following. "Let me see — there was the Young William, the Chanticleer, the Quee Vive (Qui vive), the Saucy Polly, the Hosanna, and the Horrywaur!" Of the latter I could get no explanation, until one day it flashed upon me when I was sailing out among the fleet, the "Au Revoir," belonging to a very good fellow who (according to the custom of nicknames hereabouts) goes, as I believe his father went before him, under the name of *Dickymilk*.

In-bred. "He wouldn't take off a halfpenny (discount) to-day; but offered to take off Sixpence in the Pound next month, when the stuff'll be eighteen pence dearer. That's inbred work, I call it." (The reader may call it what he pleases.)

Ivory. "The wind sprung up, and the Sea begun to show his Ivory."

Jackson. "To clap on jackson," to crowd sail; or, as it is sometimes pleasantly called "muslin."

Jenny-groats. Pearl barley.

Jill. "Just enough air to jill us along."

Joalies. Young herrings.

Joop. (A form of "Whoop," I suppose) "When those Penzance men see us go out on a Sunday, Lord! how they would joop and hallor after us." (And well they might. You Lowestoft men who go down to the West for mackerel should follow the honest custom of the country.)

Law. The wind turning so as to blow the lugger back on her nets, is said to blow "against the law."

Lipper. To curl above water, as the *rimple* of the sea, or the backs of a *skoal of fish*.

Lofty. A proper word for a *high* tide: sometimes also called "a slappin' — a ragin' — tide."

Loguy. (Query a form of *loggy?*) Heavy, slow, dull, as a ship or man.

Lowdies, or Lowders. Woodlice that eat into ship's timbers: to be trapped some think, in leaves of brake strew'd about, as flies in what they call flycatchers.

Lucky Bee. A humble, or, as we say, Bumble-bee, got out to sea, quite from his lattitude, and welcomed as a bringer of good luck if he alight on board. He is not always so tenderly used ashore, by the boys, at any rate, who, chasing him for his honey, as I was told, would pull him in two directly he was caught, *"lest he should eat up his own honey,"* if he got the chance.

Lum. The handle of an oar. To *lum* the oars, to let the handles down into the boat without unshipping them.

Kicklin'-string. On which a Warp of Herrings (apt to be as indefinite as "half a pint of Beer,") is carried, hung through the gills.

Last come Last. At last. "The old gentleman fared long upon the drope, and last come last, gave way altogether.

Macaroni. A fore-and-aft Schooner, without square yards.

Macklantan. Mackle and tan-macklintan (philologists must settle the orthography), a scanty outfit of clothes brought on board. "Well, you've brought a macklantan bundle, at any rate."

Mazy. Sickly. Herrings about to shoot the roe are said to "have the maze."

Mitten. "Dead as a Mitten" — that is the sea phrase. Another article as well appreciated by the Seaman, is commonly used for the same comparison ashore. A Gamekeeper near Lowestoft was describing how some Dignitary of the Church — he knew not what — was shooting with his master. Some game — I know not what — was sprung; and the Gamekeeper, at a loss for any correct definition of his man, called out "Blaze away, your Holiness!" — "And blowed if he didn't knock it over as dead as a Biscuit!"

Mouse To. To tie a piece of twine across the mouth of a hook. The hooks in a boat's rigging are "moused" by having a piece of twine tied across their mouths, to prevent the rolling of the boat causing them to jump out of the staples.

Mother. When a lugger does so well that another is built out of her profits, she is said to be "Mother" of the new one. Thus, by pedigrees as quaint, if not so long, as those of the Race-horses, the Linnet might be mother of the Leviathan; the Leviathan of the Little Polly; the Little Polly of the Zebedee; and Zebedee the mother of as many as you please.

Nail-sick. When a vessel begins to *complain* in that quarter. So *seamsick*, &c.

Neighbour's Fare. Doing as well as one's neighbours. "I mayn't make a fortune, but I look for neighbour's fare nevertheless."

New Year. It is thought lucky, on first going out on New Year's day, to meet "a big man"; not big in paunch, but in height and breadth, and all the noble proportions "that may become a man." Lowestoft is a lucky place to live in for this; provided there be not many French Luggers in the port nor many of the young English "Quality" at the lodgings. But it is not the time of year for them.

Old. "An old wind," &c.

I have not been able to discover the history of one member of this most ancient family. "Old Gooseberry," I know; and "Old Sarah," I know; but who is "Old Boots?" he is well known in these parts, too. "Only let me clap a taups'l (topsail) on, and I'll run away from him like "Old Boots.""

Perry Wind.; half a gale.

Paper-stuff. "Why, her spars and taikle (tackle) was only so much paper-stuff; in a manner of speaking."

Pea-soup. "Regular as pea-soup" — a figure from the Navy, I suppose.

Pencil-work. "His room is swept as clean as pencil-work."

Poker Beer. Beer heated with a red-hot poker; about a pint to a poker, I am told. There are worse things, and as Lamb said, better.

Proud. Tight or *taught*. "That rope is rather *proud*."

Proud as a Horse. The Sailor generally regarding that creature as showing so much of the Devil, with all its tearings, prancings, and "Ha Ha's!" The Landsman may retort that the Sailor's *Rocking-horse* is quite as unruly a beast, plunging, snorting, foaming and carrying itself and rider to the bottom.

Prudent. I have heard this word thus oddly used concerning a ship. "That old Polly is scarce prudent to go to sea; "*sc*. sea worthy.

Puff the Gaff. To blow a secret. "He thought to get off clear but his mate puffed the gagg, and they were soon after him." This phrase calls for a nautical philologist.

Punt. The Lowestoft lug-sailed long-shore boat.

Raffle. The tackle, spars, &c. of a ship.

Red Caps. Formerly, I am told, the Master-boat among the Luggers; she that has raised most money by the voyage, distinguished her crew with red caps in token of victory.

Reign. To continue in use. "The Hebe was an old ship ten years ago; but she *reign* still, I *hare*."

Rind. Skin and Bone; "A mere rind of a woman."

Rippier. "One who brings fish from the coast to sell inland.

Rixy. The smallest of the sea-gulls. Tern?

Rooms. The spaces between a boat's thwarts; thus divided, and named; I, Fore-peak; 2, Fore-room; 3, Well; 4, After-room.

Safer. A freight of fish. "A good safer of mackerel, herring," &c.

Saltwagin'. So pronounced (if not *solwagin'*) from, perhaps, an indistinct implication of *salt* (water), and *wages. Salvaging*, of course.

Samp. To lull; sea or wind. "When the wind samped a little," &c.

Scandalized. To lower the peak of a schooner's mainsail! At any rate, when the sail is so left, she is said to have "her mainsail Scandalised." How could my friends have thought of this word, for the purpose? And yet, there is something in the *shape* of the word.

Scroper. A salwagin smack.

Shies. The palisades fixed on the beach to withstand the encroachments of the sea about Felixstowe.

Ship's Husband; who lays in stores of provisions for the ship. This sounds a fine old term; I dare say it is not peculiar to us, but I have not happened on it in print.

Shittle Nets. Nets that have become rolled over and over like a cocoon, whether by tide or sea, at wind as they are drying ashore.

Shut the Door After Him; as a willock diving, or a man drowning.

Shreep. To clear away partially; as mist, &c.

Smigs. Small fry of herring, mackerel, eels, &c.

Soldier. A red herring; or the remainder Tobacco in a pipe. "I say, just wait till I've smoked this Soldier out."

Samson-post. The pedestal post of the mast from deck to keelson.

Shottener. A shotten herring.

Smell the Ground. A vessel, I am told, loses the control of her helm in proportion as she nears the ground; and so is said "to smell it."

Solomon-gundy. Salmagundi, of course; made of pickled herring, minced up raw with pepper, vinegar, &c.

Spoom. To send before the wind.

Standard. What has worn a long while; an old man; old horse; old coat; old boat, &c. "That's a standard, I warrant."

Stove Down. "There was an old Gannet a watchin' us aloft; so I threw him a Mackerel; he turned his old eye upon it, and *stove down*, and clean'd him off in a wink." Qy. from what verb?

Stifler. "He's a head-stifler at our club, I assure you." Head man; leader.

Stocker Fish. Refuse, such as thornback, roker, gurnet, &c., given to the apprentices on board smacks at their perquisite.

Stull. An extra-large mackerel.

There is a word for the Philologist. Can it have to do with "stalwart", of whose derivation the dictionaries make odd work.

Sprat's Eye. A sixpence; but this surely was between the days of the ancient and modern Groat.

Swattock. "She" — a skittish ship —" took me right off my legs, and brought me down a rare *swattock* on deck.

Tabernacle. The receptacle for a mast.

Three-sticker. Salwagee for any three-masted ship; thrice blest, if she be, or promise to be, in trouble.

Toeing it and Heeling it. A vessel pitching in the sea.

Tom Tailor. By this name is the Mother Carey's chickens known in those seas.

Torch Up. "Once the wood is kindled it'll soon torch up." Not so bad.

Tow. (Rhyming to now); nets. "Those over-grown luggers pull so hard on their tow, they tear it all to pieces."

Trap-handed. Deceitful. "A trap-handed fellow." not so bad, neither.

Trim-tram. The Yarmouth fore-and aft 'long-shore fishing boat.

Twy; Twoy; or Twoyte. To slew round, or become disengaged from any stoppage. "There she twoy!"

Wake Up. A vessel beginning to stir herself with a fresh air, after drowsy going. She then begins *to talk* also; and, still more lively, proceeds to "pick up her crumbs."

Weep. The nails weeping with rust is one sign of the ship's *complaining.*

Whole Water. Deep water, as opposed to "broken water", which is shallow.

Willock. A guillemont, I am told.

The same bird that, after "shutting the door after him," presents the kitty with the fish he has re-appeared with. This is not the action of an ill-mannered bird; nor have I seen anything at all wild in his demeanour. Yet they say, "mad as a willock;" as we on shore say with equal propriety, "mad as a hatter."

In the reference library at Ipswich is a beautifully written manuscript of a couple of letters sent to Major Moor on the appearance of his Vocabulary. They offer amendments and one or two other examples, two of which are mere malapropisms and not specimens of local dialect. This little book dates from 1823. I give a few of the words.

Insistance = Assistant. "Such a Surgeon did not call to-day, but his Insistance came in his stead."

Projection = Objection. An old woman said to me "No Sir, I have no projection whatsoever."

Nuffle To get down to the bottom of the bed and there to lie nose and knees together, is to nuffle.

Rile. If you don't let me alone you'll rile my blood."

Spend. Pork in Suffolk fed upon beans only, is generally affirmed not to spend well; that is to say, it boils away and therefore is unprofitable.

Spawn. Spoken contemptuosly of any boy or child. "A regular little nasty spawn."

Streeky. "I fare quite streaky to-day," that is I am troubled with shifting rheumatic pains.

Sound as a Roach. The roach sleeps soundly on the surface of the water.

Dan Scarf. "I can't keep the dan off that child's head."

Hard Beer = Beer when nearly sour.

Guden. 'Yes sir, but she'll want great guden up afore she git about.'

14

Dunwich, East Anglia's Lost Capital

Low and loud and long, a voice for ever,
　　Sounds the wind's clear story like a song.
Tomb from tomb the waves devouring sever,
　　Dust from dust as years relapse along;
Graves where men made sure to rest, and never
　　Lie dismantled by the season's wrong.

Swinburne

The story of Dunwich really is that of its river, the Blyth, which rises near Laxfield and Cratfield and flows fifteen miles through the old Blything Hundred to the sea south of Southwold. The river name means blithe or pleasant, and is an old one. Originally the mouth was southwards of its present position, but northwards of the old city of Dunwich, which was in reality somewhat inland.

When the Neolithic subsidence took place and England became detached from the Continent, the river valleys were formed and the spot which came to be known as Dunwich appeared. The then East Anglian coastline must have presented a very ragged appearance, with deep inlets and jutting promontories. Successive gales and scouring tides must have attacked these soft headlands and cut them back quickly and effectively.

The prevailing drift along this shore has been always from north to south, and the outlets of all the rivers have suffered from this southward action of shifting shingle becoming dead, and forming itself into banks and spits. The inhabitants of Yarmouth were much put about by the constant shifting of their haven's mouth, so that during the course of the centuries various cuts were made through the spit to bring the mouth nearer the town. A gatway was cut in 1392, at the north end of Gorleston, and five others were cut before the present mouth was fixed in 1566. This same action of the tides was responsible for closing the smaller outlets in Suffolk, such as Kessingland, Benacre,

Minsmere and the Little Hundred river at Thorpe. And, of
course, the present outlet of the Waveney is artificial.

The Dunwich river was no exception, but the constant
efforts of its inhabitants, unlike those of Yarmouth and
Lowestoft, proved of no avail. The longshore drift proved
too strong and the tides prevailed. What happened here can
be seen to-day at Orford, which is a harbour enclosed by a
gigantic shingle spit deflecting the mouth of the Alde for
some eleven miles. This varies in width from about fifty
yards at Slaughden to nearly half a mile at Orford Ness.
The record of Dunwich is one of woe and dismay as the
new mouths were cut and lost, until by erosion the famous
old port ceased to function and was at last lost to
Southwold.

The original extent of Dunwich must have been considerable, always bearing in mind that a medieval city was not
large and that London was originally contained within a
square mile. Tradition has it that a forest called Eastwood
stretched several miles south-east of the town, but was
early devoured by the sea. Another called Westwood (evidently surviving today in the ancient manor of that name
at Blythburgh) stood westerly of and contiguous to the
forest of Eastwood. In those thickets the Conqueror gave
leave to the Rouses of Badingham and other nobility to
hunt and hawk. Another tradition says there was a patent
to the Scriveners to hunt in a forest fifteen miles east of
Dunwich. Be that as it may, these traditions suggest wide
boundaries. Gardner, the local historian, considered that the
land must have stretched far out, providing the south
cheek, as Easton Ness the north cheek of the sinus of
Solebay.

Further confirmation of this Eastwood came to light in
1739, during a great storm, when the roots of many trees,
which may have been the last remnant of that forest were
uncovered, a more picturesque tradition, and one worthy of
Beatrix Potter, was that the tailors of Dunwich could sit in
their shops and see the shipping at anchor in the Yarmouth
roads.

All Saints' Church, Dunwich, 1785

Bramfield Church from the south-east (from Suckling's *History of Suffolk*)

The Sole Bay Fight, from the painting in Greenwich Hospital.
Van Ghent's ships attack the *Royal James*

In an article on the Suffolk shore by J.A. Steers in the *Proceedings of the Suffolk Institute of Archaeology*, Vol. XIX, the writer suggest that the loss of land since Neolithic times was about two miles. Against that is a personal experience of a local fisherman recorded in the *East Anglian Miscellany* for 1919: "It might interest you to know that in 1884 a Southwold Trawl boat came fast to what they thought was a wreck in 10½ fathoms of water, Dunwich Church (open), which means we could see through the two old belfry windows of old All Saints, then standing. We reckoned at the time we were roughly about 3½ miles from the shore, the masonry had some of the old Roman shallow bricks in it, that our forefathers used to work in with others, and they laid on the beach at the foot of the Gunhill (Southwold) all that summer."

The position of Dunwich at the time of its rise to power was that of an inland port, nicely protected from the ravages of the sea. This can be seen to some extent in the map published in Gardner's *Dunwich*. But it must be remembered that this, if accurate, is of later-day draughts-manship.

It is almost certain that Dunwich, situated as it is about midway along the Suffolk coast, was a Roman station. If one considers the coast as coming within the defensive survey of the Roman occupiers, the circumstantial evidence would point to this. With Burgh Castle to the north and the supposed Walton Castle to the south, it would be difficult not to believe that such was the case; that here at least was a signal station, part of the coastal defences under the charge of the Count of the Saxon Shore.

Confirmation of the Roman occupation has not been lacking. The chief find was at Scotts Hall, when a coarse earthenware pot, some eight to ten inches high and half an inch thick, was dug up. This contained silver and brass coins of the Roman era, although too decayed to be identified. Another smaller pot nearby was empty. Two other objects found at Dunwich form part of the Acton Collection at Moyses Hall, Bury St Edmunds. They are described as chapes (part of a scabbard). A number of Roman coins have been found on the beach after the 'scouring tides' that take place in January.

Dunwich spelt Donewic, Duneuuic, a trisyllabic form representing the Anglo-Saxon Dunan-wic, i.e. 'Duna's village' The name Duna occurs in Dunan-Heafod and Dunan-Hyl. It is possible that the name was suggested by an older one. Beda Hist. Eccl. 11. 15 has "*in civitate Domnoc*," for which the A.S. version has "*on Dommo-ceastre*". Domnoc is not English, but may be Celtic. In fact we are told that it is so in McClure's *British Place Names*, p. 173, note I, where it is said that Dumna involves a term meaning 'deep', with -oc as an adjectival termination; i.e. (as I suppose) the sense is 'deepish'; and it signifies 'a port with a deep water approach'. The base is the Indo-germanic *Dubnos Dumnos*, 'deep', whence the Old Irish *fu-domain*, 'deep.', Welsh *dwfn* (fem. *dofn*.

Professor W.W. Skeat, *The Place Names of Suffolk*, 1913.

When the Roman occupation began to thin out and the raids of the Picts and Scots grew more dangerous, it was evident that the Romans called to their aid Angle mercenaries from Schleswig-Holstein, and Saxons from the area between the Elbe and the Weser in north-west Germany. These were the originators of the Anglo-Saxon communities which later were to dominate this part of England and to provide the most fascinating chapter in the history of East Anglia. Those who made their homes north of the Waveney called themselves North Folk, while those who remained between the Waveney and the Stour, became known as the South Folk. And Suffolk was born.

During the first four centuries of this era various raiders made their presence felt and were assimilated into the scheme of things, while about A.D. 500 other arrivals came from northern Jutland, to which part they had migrated from southern Sweden. It was this tribe that provided East Anglia with a family known as the Wuffingas, a cadet of which house Sigebert, was to make Dunwich his capital. With him the Dunwich story really begins.

This dynasty was founded c. 525 by Wehha, described

by Nennius as the first king "who reigned in Britain over the East Angles". He was succeeded by his son Wuffa or Uffa; next came Tyttla, who had two sons Redwald and Ene, but only the former ascended the throne.

Redwald was the most illustrious of these monarchs, attaining to the eminence of Bretwalda, or overlord, of the other kingdoms of the Saxon heptarchy. He was succeeded by his second son, Eorpwald, who was murdered about 628. He was succeeded by his cousin or step-brother, Sigebert, who had been living in exile in Gaul, and, as he chose to land at the port of Dunwich and there set up his kingdom, he came not merely to claim a throne and to succeed his murdered kinsman, but to secure the conversion of his homeland, for he himself had embraced Christianity whilst an exile at the Frankish court. According to Bede . . . Sigbert, brother of the same Eorpwald, took the kingdom, a man in all points most Christian and revered, who while his brother was yet alive, living banished in France, was instructed in the mysteries of the faith; of which he went about to make all his realm partake as soon as he began to reign."

Sigebert is said to have built himself a palace at Dunwich, but it is doubtful if he created a mint there, because no coins have ever been found that could be ascribed to this origin. Besides, as R. Rainbird Clarke has pointed out, the first inscribed coins that can be attributed to a specific East Anglian monarch are those bearing the name of Athelstan I, who reigned c. 825-40, and of his successor Elthelweard.

King Sigebert was somewhat of a reluctant monarch, and soon after he had established himself he retired to the monastery at Bury St Edmunds, which he founded about 637, leaving the affairs of state to his brother Ecric. When the pagan king of Mercia, Penda, invaded his kingdom, Siegbert's people called upon him to lead them against the invader, "in faith that his presence would bring them the favour of heaven". He was not loath to obey the summons, yet, being more inclined to sainthood than soldiering, he armed himself with a wand only, and was slain, leading his people; and his brother Ecric with him.'

The line now passed in succession to three sons of Redwald's brother, Ene, who himself, be it noted, did not succeed. The first of these was the saintly Anna (d. 654), who was father to five sainted persons: Jurmin, his son; St Etheldreda, born at Exning, near Newmarket, and enshrined in the work of Alan of Walsingham at Ely; St Ethelburga of Faremoutier in France, where she founded a monastery; Sexburga, who became queen of Kent; and Withburga of East Dereham, whose perennial well of healing water is to be found beside the detached steeple of that village church. The legendary white doe which furnished her with milk is to be seen on some of those famous Norfolk screens.

Anna reigned some nineteen years, but tribal war, waged again by Penda, brought his life to a close on the battle-field of Bulcamp, almost within sight of Dunwich. With him perished his son, Jurmin, and the two bodies were alleged to have been buried within the nearby church at Blythburgh. For long enough a plain tomb was pointed out as as that of Anna's. However that may be, it is reasonably certain that Jurmin's body did rest there. M.R. James in his *Suffolk and Norfolk*, states that this body was removed to the great monastic house of Bury St Edmunds in the eleventh century, much to the disgust of the people of Blythburgh, and that it was housed at or near the Chapel of the Virgin in the central apse of the abbey church, in a silver shrine; and remained there until the Dissolution. It would have figured in the great processions. St Jurmin (often miswritten Germanus or Firminius) was com-memorated on 23rd February and 31st May.

Aethelhere's reign was brief enough, lasting only one year, from the battle of Blythburgh (654) to that of Winwaed in Yorkshire in 655. He was succeeded by another brother, Aethelwald (655-664), who was a christian. He was succeeded by Aldwulf, son of Aethelhere, a contemporary of Bede, who died in 713, and was in turn succeeded by two sons: Aelwald who died in 740; and Elric, with whom the dynasty came to an end.

To return to Sigebert — soon after his arrival in Dunwich he was followed by Felix, a Burgundian missionary monk whom he had met in Gaul. To quote further from Bede.

> Whose good endeavours herein, Bishop Felix fathered to his great glory, and when Felix came from the coasts of Burgundy (where he was born and took holy orders), to Honorious the Archbishop and had opened his longing unto him, the Archbishop sent him to preach the word of life to the aforesaid nation of the East English. Where certes his desires fell not in vain; nay rather this good husbandman of the spiritual soil found in that nation manifest fruit of people that believed.
>
> For according to the good abodement of his name he brought all that province now delivered from their long iniquity and unhappiness, unto faith and works of justice and the gifts of unending happiness; and he had ruled the same province seventeen years in that dignity, he ended his life in peace in that same place.

It may be here stated that Felix died on the 8th March 647. If he was buried in Dunwich his remains were shortly removed to Soham, a village in the Isle of Ely, where he had founded a monastery. As this was later pillaged by the Danes, Etheric, a faithful monk, took the body to another abbey at Ramsey, Hunts, where Ethelstone the abbot had it solemnly interred.

It has been conjectured that Sigebert built a church for St Felix in Dunwich, which from the foregoing would have been only natural. Scholars have gone so far as to dispute this. If it was a new building, then it would have been of simple construction; but it may well have been a converted pagan shrine, perchance left by the Romans and dedicated to Mithras.

Sigebert appears to have met Felix whilst he was in exile, but how he came to know Fursey is not known. However, he had not been established as king very long when Fursey made his way into his kingdom.

Fursa, in Latin Furseus, in English Fursey, was an Irishman of noble birth, his father being Fintan, the son of Finlog, an under-king in South Munster, and his mother Gelges, daughter of Aedh Finn, a prince in Connaught. He spent several years in Suffolk, preaching and converting some of the inhabitants. Moreover, he founded a monastery, or at least a cell, on land granted to him by Sigebert in the Roman fortress of Burgh (Cnobberesburgh). Excavations made in 1958 revealed traces of this establishment when post-holes and painted wall-plates were found. Still further confirmation was contained in a note in the *Daily Telegraph* of 8th February, 1962: "Traces of what are believed to be cells of a Saxon monastery founded about A.D. 635 have been discovered at Burgh Castle, Suffolk. The find, consisting of the foundations of circular wattle and daub huts, was made by a Ministry of Works excavator".

From the foregoing it will be seen that in the space of a few years Dunwich had become a centre of life and light, closely associated with the Wuffinga kings, that was to knit the countryside into a subsequent united kingdom. It is not too much to say, with Suckling in his *History*, that during the Saxon era Dunwich was at the period of its highest dignity and importance, though not of its commercial prosperity and wealth. Before 670 there were at least five monasteries: one founded by Felix at Soham, St. Fursey's at Burgh Castle, Sigebert's at Bury, Anna's at Blythburgh, and St Botolph's at Ikanhoe. This spread of monasticism brought with it literacy and devotion to the scholarship for which the Anglo-Saxon church became justly famous, although a whalebone writing tablet for the monastery of Blythburgh is the sole survivor from this area.

We now come to the Domesday Book; the entries for Dunwich are to be found in the second volume, which is the smaller of the two. From the colophon the survey was probably commenced in 1085 and completed in 1086. Six towns in the county possessed burgesses, of which Dunwich heads the list with 316. There is one main entry and two or three subsidiary entries.

East Anglia supported an infinitely larger population than ever before, and must be reckoned as one of the most densely populated regions in Britain. That, in spite of the Danish invasion. Dunwich boasted something like three thousand inhabitants. The entries as translated by Lord J.W.N. Hervey are as follows:

Edric of Laxfield held in Dunwich in King Edward's time as a manor — and now Robert Malet holds it. Then 2 carucates of land, now 1. The sea carried away the other. And always 1 plough team in demesne. Then 12 Bordars, now 2. Then a church now 3: and they render 4 pounds and 10 shillings. And altogether it is valued at 50 pounds, and 60,000 herrings by way of a gift. And in King Edward's time it rendered 10 pounds.

And moreover Robert de Vallibus holds 1 acre of land, valued at 8 pence. And Norman holds 1 acre valued at 2/8. And Gilbert the Blond holds four score men — and they render 4 pounds and 8 thousand herrings of this said Robert.

The king has in Dunwich the custom following, that two or three shall go to the Hundred if they shall have been duly warned. And if they do not do this they shall make forefeiture of 2 ores. And if a thief is caught there he shall be brought to trial — And corporal punishment he shall receive in Bliburgh. And his pecuniary fine remains to the lord of Dunwich. And in King Edward's time there was no exchange therein, but at Blithburgh.

Dunwich was granted to Robert Malet by the Conqueror, but when later he was deprived of his estates and banished the kingdom, Dunwich became a royal demesne under the Crown. Nothing more is heard until the reign of Henry II, when William of Newberry described it as "a towne of good note, abounding with much riches and sundry kinds of merchandise". The fee-farm had grown to £120 3s. 4d. and 24,000 herrings. Indeed, the prosperity of the town had so far advanced as to allow it to make a contribution of £133 6s. 8d to the marriage of Maud, the King's eldest daughter, to Henry the Lion, Duke of Saxony; whereas Ipswich only contributed £55 6s. 8d. However, the town was heavily fortified at this time as Prince Henry and his brother discovered when they waged a war against their father. They essayed to take it by land but withdrew.

Moving to the reign of Edward II (1307-27), what was described as a "Topographical Curiosity" appeared in the *Gentleman's Magazine*, for January 1862 from a manuscript of this period. It contains a list of about a hundred places in England, with the character for which each place was celebrated. For instance, Cornwall for tin, Oxford for schools. Dunwich was noted for its mills — "Molins de Donesqyz," Dunwich mills. This would suggest a high state of agriculture in the vicinity and the ability of the town to export corn. It is clear also from an ancient deed of a "Grant by Eglinus, prior of Snape, to Wimund the Chaplain, of the perpetual vicarage of Frestune (Friston) Church paying yearly 16s. and 2 lbs of Wax, *Dunwich weight*. Witnesses, — John the Chaplain of Aldeburgh, Roger the Chaplain of Lestune, William de Glanvill," and others. Did, therefore, Dunwich have a bushel measure as other large towns such as Winchester?

Dunwich sided with King John (1199-1216) in his dispute with the barons and fitted out several ships on his behalf. It was, in fact, in 1205 that the first Station List of the King's Ships was made, and some idea of the greatness to which Dunwich had risen may be gathered from the fact that there were two galleys at Ipswich, but no less than five at Dunwich, which was the same number as at London.

In recognition of their loyalty in the first year of his reign, the King granted Dunwich its first and greatest charter, creating the town a free borough, and bestowing tremendous privileges on the citizens, with "soc and sac, wreck and lagan" (goods lying at the bottom of the sea, lost by shipwreck, which by ancient laws belonged to the Lord High Admiral); and exempting them from certain tolls and customs. A second charter was granted in the king's tenth year.

Dunwich had reason to feel grateful to this very wily monarch, and it is reported that he visited here in 1216. In

1215 he confirmed his first charter. In so doing he vested the government of the town in a mayor and four bailiffs or sheriffs, in the place of the portreeve who had previously governed. The third or 1215 charter is still in existence, having been pursued and retrieved by the late E.R. Cooper after it had disappeared.

Henry III (1216-72) remitted £20 pounds of the farm rent and made a gift of £47 10s. towards renewing and repairing the port. An attempt was made at this time to move the outlet, which evidently ran through the domains of one William Helmeth, who was causing trouble by exacting fourpence from every ship, without the licence of the King. The charter was renewed by Henry in his fortieth year.

This was an era of considerable national disturbance; Henry had one political absorption and that was to recover the continental dominion of his predecessors. However, it is during this reign that Dunwich, of all the Suffolk ports, stands out pre-eminently as being the one upon which the Crown could rely upon as always having ships and men available. In 1235, when most of the Cinque Ports, together with Yarmouth and Southampton, were assessed for one ship each, Dunwich alone was required to send two.

Dunwich at this time was often coupled with the Cinque Ports, and when Henry was defeated at Taillebourgh in 1242, he urged the bailiffs of Dunwich, in company with the Cinque Ports, to devote their whole strength to ravage the French coast and destroy French commerce. He is also reputed to have paid Dunwich £15 for services rendered by the town to his father.

Edward I (1272-1307) confirmed the previous charters in his seventh and thirteenth years, and remitted the sum of £200 which his father had lent them. At this time the town is reported to have possessed a fleet of eleven ships of war, sixteen fishing ships, twenty barques or vessels trading to the North Sea and Iceland, and twenty-four small boats for the home fishing.

In 1294 the town furnished eleven ships for service in

Gascony, which sailed from Plymouth with the King's brother Edmund, Earl of Leicester and Lancaster, and remained there from St Andrew's day to the Feast of Pentecost. During this period they lost four ships which were the subject of a claim.

In the reign of Edward II (1307-27) no charters appear to have been granted, but a mandate was given to John Howard, Sheriff of Suffolk, prohibiting the sale of all goods, merchandise and fish imported at the new port, except at the ancient market place at Dunwich, on forfeiture of the goods etc. so vended. This was granted to retrieve the loss sustained by the town in consequence of the old port having been obstructed by the sea and a new one opened at Blythburgh.

We now come to the long reign of Edward III (1327-77), who renewed the charter in the third year of his reign, and reduced the Farm Rent to £14 10s. 9d. However, trouble was overtaking Dunwich apace. On 14th January 1328, the port was so choked by the north-east winds that all the means used for its recovery proved ineffectual. Later a portion of the town was lost with four hundred houses, shops and windmills. In 1347 Dunwich sent six ships with 102 mariners to assist the king at Calais, but they were apparently lost with five hundred seamen and stores to the value of £1,000.

Here follows a list of nine Dunwich ships which assembled at Goseford (Bawdsey), June 1338, for the king's expedition to Flanders. This was collected by the late V.B. Redstone.

Ship	Master	Men	Pay for 27 days
Rode Cogge	Roger Hode	43	£15 . 3. 9d
Godbefor	Andrew Litester	40	£14. 3. 6d
Sentemariebot	William Tutepeny	31	£11. 16 1d
Godyer	John Tutepeny	31	£11. 2. 9d
Welfare	John Frese sen.	31	£11. 2. 9d
Margarete	Stephen Batman	23	£ 8. 12. 1½
Katherine	William Crele	20	£ 7. 11. 10½

| Margaret | Edward Sorel | 15 | £ 5. 11. 4½ |
| Plente | Stephen Ferese | 28 | £10. 5. 10½ |

In the succeeding reign of Richard II (1377-99), Dunwich moved a long way towards its final overthrow, when, on the night of 1st January 1386, a great storm swept away the churches of Sts Leonard, Martin and Nicholas and washed away the shore close to the convent of Black Friars.

This brings us to the reign of Henry IV (1399-1413). The charter was again confirmed in the ninth year of the reign, but an action of far-reaching effect to Dunwich brought against Robert Swillynton was now heard. It appears that Robert Swillynton, knight, and Roger his son, claimed the revenue of the port for Southwold, and Dunwich lost the case.

Henry V reigned for nine years (1413-22) and the charter was renewed in the last year of his reign. A big fleet was required for Henry's passage to France in 1417, Dunwich sending one vessel.

This brings us to the reign of Henry VI (1422-61), which saw the farm reduced to £12 2s. 1d., plus 3s. 4d per annum demanded by Sir Roger Swillynton of Blythburgh.

The succeeding reign, that of Edward IV (1461-83), brings us to the Wars of the Roses, when Dunwich decided in favour of the King. As a reward, on 4th July 1463, the charter was confirmed and certain liberties were granted to the town.

Passing over the murder of Edward V, and the short reign of Richard III, brings us to Henry VII (1485-1509), who, as a punishment to Dunwich for participating on the side of the 'White', incorporated Southwold. This led to the growth of this town and the final dissolution of Dunwich. However, when the Earl of Surrey invaded Scotland in 1497, and Suffolk ships were required as transports, Dunwich provided two.

We now come to the reign of Henry VIII (1509-47),

which ushered in an important era for Dunwich, as for other cities of England. For Dunwich in that Henry may be considered as the father of the British Navy. Impressment of shipping may be said to have ceased, but not so the impressment of men, and Dunwich was called upon, in company with adjacent ports to provide shipwrights and caulkers to proceed to the new dockyard at Woolwich. Then, of course, Dunwich would have suffered by reason of the suppression of the monasteries, in the decrease of demand for fish and the like requirements of the religious houses.

Passing over the reign of Edward VI (1547-52), brings us to that of Mary (1553-9). She issued forth from neighbouring Framlingham to place a bloody hand on England. Two martyrs perished at nearby Yoxford: A. Shearman and Roger Coo, "an aged man and full of faith".

We now come to the reign of Elizabeth I (1559-1603). This era, which meant so much to England, was but a sunset to Dunwich. However, the charter was renewed in the first year of her reign. It is given in full in Gardner's *History*.

In spite of royal favours, the town was by this time reduced to about a quarter of its original size, and was in considerable poverty. The Queen, in her carefulness, lent the town a sum of money which was obtained from the sale of bells, lead, iron, glass and stone, from Ingate church, Beccles, the proceeds of which amounted to £76 18s. 4d; also lead from the chancel of the church at Kessingland which was pulled down.

In 1570 two of the main gateways of the old town were engulfed, the gilden and south gates, and the old port was said to have suffered "incredible damage". Again in 1589 the port was choked, which left only a narrow channel, known as Hummerston's Cut, which was highly dangerous to navigate owing to the treacherous Passely Sands. This cut cost £300 to construct and almost impoverished the town. The entrance to the haven is described by Gardner as being on the north side of the town and ran by Walberswick to Dunwich. This by reason of shoals and loose sand with the liability of shifting, gave occasion to the mariners of those days to remark:

> Dunwich, Soul and Walserwig,
> All go in at a lowsy Crick.

One of the most carefully watched possessions at this time of the threatened Armada, must have been the beacon. This stood on a hill of that name south of the town. The Conder, or Conner, probably used as a lighthouse, was erected at Cock Hill.

In May 1575 Thomas Cowper, bailiff of the town 1560, 1566, 1568 and 1572, made his last will and testament, "beinge very perfecte in memory and yet visited with the visitation of Almighty God in bodie". He left his "shippe or Fissher called the Herene, his half part of the ship Espery, his little cocke-boate and his herring and spurling nets, and £5, unto the use of the key of this towne, and his dwelling house to his son Michael, on condition that he should dwell therein."

It may well be that hardly a vestige of that Elizabethan Dunwich remains today, unless it is the cottage in the Street. This is reputed to be the old town hall, successor to the one that stood in the market square and was washed away by the tide. Here the last mayors were elected and carried past in procession, as from 'time out of mind.'

James I (1603-25) was proclaimed in Dunwich by Thomas Rous, Esq., on 31st March, with due pomp and ceremony. Sixteen hundred and eight saw the High Road to the sea eaten away and another made through Peter Willet's ground. James saw fit to renew the charter.

Dunwich Annual Fair for the sale of Pedlery, was held on 25th July. This festival was followed in 1616 by a sad occurence, which must have cast considerable gloom over the whole district. Twenty-two people from Southwold, who had visited the fair were returning to their town by water when their boat fouled a cable holding another vessel to Southwold quay and they were all drowned. Amongst them were Edward and Elizabeth Yonges, son and daughter of Christhofer Yonges, vicar of Southwold.

This brings us to the ill-fated reign of Charles I (1625-49), when shipping is again the principal item of interest; but now it is for fishing rather than naval engagements. Neither should we forget that very apt bit of description of this hazardous occupation, "adventurers in the fishing trade".

The Mariner's Mirror for April 1939, contains a transcript account for a voyage to Iceland for ling, etc., made by the *Jamys* of Dunwich in 1545-6; this was contributed by the late E.R. Cooper. The list of goods taken on board is extremely interesting. The first item is for salt: "15 wey and a hauf at 36/8 the wey = £28. 18s. 4d". This is quickly followed by "44 butz of bier at 13/4 the butz". Then follows flour, biscuits, cheese, tallow, rossen, oatmeal, bread, pitch, tar, "boetankers, A1 kynd of nayls", gutting and splitting knives, honey, lanterns, compasses and candles. Then comes the men's wages, "of this present viage". The 'master under God', one Sanders of Dunwich, including his servant, £11. The master's mate £5 13s. 4d., while the men's wages varied from £2. 10s. 0d. to 36s. 8d., most receiving 46s. 8d. One interesting item is this section of the accounts is "In godspens when they were hieryed 2/-". This is a reference to the 'godspenny' or earnest money, in token of the bargain made to serve and extremely binding in those days. It would appear these trips to Iceland and the Faroes were two-way voyages of great value. Goods were taken on the outward journey to be disposed of to the natives at considerable profit. These included copper "kyttels, lynnen of all sorts, two tonne of wynne, 16 yards of broyd clothe and a dozen schyrtes".

Convoys were in fashion, as in the two world wars, and these fishing fleets were 'wafted' by His Majesty's ships.

Otherwise it meant certain destruction by pirates or enemy vessels. Then, as always, grievances were found in the bad staff work, and the ill timing of the arrangements made for the sailings.

We now come to the Commonwealth period (1649-60), and the outbreak of the Dutch War. This is a space of time in which Dunwich often appears in the official records, but purely in a passive capacity. Curiously enough the only token attributed to Dunwich belongs to this time, viz.:

O. IOHN. WHITMAN — I.F.W.
R. OF DVNWICH) I.F.W.

On the obverse the bottom of the I of IOHN is between the mint mark and the top of the W in the field. On another as above, but the obverse of a different die, the bottom of the I the other side of the W to the mint mark. (From Golding's *Coinage of Suffolk.*)

The Fleet was for long at anchor off Dunwich and the adjacent ports, and there was much coming and going to the mainland; but the time for sending ships and men from this brave old port had passed. Though in all probability some of its fishermen were impressed into the navy to meet van Tromp. One of the ships constantly referred to was *The Resolution.*

This brings us to the Restoration and Charles II (1660-85), with the Fleet still off Dunwich. One of the first acts of the new monarch was to reduce the farm rent to £5 per annum. This shows how low Dunwich had fallen; and it was only with great difficulty that this was paid. It was bestowed on Queen Catherine as part of her jointure. In 1677 the sea reached the market place and the old market cross was taken down by the inhabitants and the lead sold. The proceeds seem to have been used for the building of shops for the convenience of the market. By 1680 all buildings north of Maison Dieu were demolished.

Fourth of December 1669:

Silas Taylor to Williamson. The storm on Sunday night forced one of the Harwich packet boats aground near Dunwich and broke her back. The master sent the mail from thence: all have deserted the ship.

Whereas His Majesty was pleased in the year 1672 to be at the charge of making waterworks on the north side of Dunwich co. Suffolk within a furlong of the High Water-mark, so that the ground, being level, casks may be rolled to and fro; and for the better direction to it, there is a white post set up as a landmark. These are therefore, to inform all Masters of ships, who shall ride in the Bay of Dunwich now lately called Sole Bay that they may be supplied with good fresh water, proportionate to their bulk or occasion, for which water nothing is to be paid, the work being made at His Majesty's proper cost, for the benefit of Seamen.

In 1672, as a direct result of the Declaration of Indulgence passed this year, Mrs Dinnington applied for a licence to permit her house in Dunwich to be used as a Congregational preaching place. It would appear that the local minister was Edmund Whincop, M.A., who resided in Middleton.

We now come to the reign of Queen Anne (1702-14), and it is interesting to note that one of the ships of Her Majesty's Navy in 1705, was the *Dunwich*. A Phillipa Elliot, widow of Captain Christopher Elliot, commander of that vessel, petitioned the Lord High Treasurer for recompence for his loss, he being very much wounded at Vigo, in the hottest part of that service, though he was the only sea captain wounded. He was in charge of the 'Granado bomb'.

The *Dunwich* was built at Shoreham, Sussex, in 1695, of 250 tons and twenty-four guns. She was at the abortive attack on Cadiz in 1702, and from thence sailed for Vigo, where she captured a Spanish vessel which confirmed the news that the French and Spanish Fleets were in Vigo. Admiral Rooke attacked on the 12th October 1702, broke the boom and captured fifteen warships and eight galleons, five being sunk. The *Dunwich* was in the thick of this fight. She was eventually sunk as a foundation at Plymouth in 1704, and her name was not repeated.

The following is of interest, particularly as it is a reminder of the Test Act, repealed 1828. This John Battley was a Member of Parliament for Dunwich in 1706 and again in 1708. "We, Robert Hacon, clerk, minister of the Parish and Parish Church of Donwich in the county of Suffolk and Gabriel Eade, church-warden of the same Parish and Parish Church, do hereby certify that John Battley of Donwich in the said county of Suffolk, Gent., upon the Lord's Day commonly called Sunday, the thirteenth day of November last immediately after Divine Service and sermon did in the parish church aforesaid receive the Sacraments of the Lord's Supper according to the custom of the Church of England. In the witness whereof we have hereunto subscribed our hands the twenty fourth day of December in the year of our Lord, One thousand seven hundred and eight."

In the time of George I (1714-27) Charles Long petitioned in 1718 for a grant for thirty-one years of the farm at £5 per annum, but it was not granted. It would appear, however, that Sir George Downing was more successful and obtained it at the same fee for ninety-nine years.

At the height of its prosperity Dunwich possessed a daily market, which later became a weekly market, held on Saturdays. Kirby, however, in his *Suffolk Traveller* states: " . . . it hath a mean market on Mondays". There were two fairs, that of St Leonard's, held 5th, 6th and 7th November; and St James' Fair, held in the street of that name on 25th July. This latter is reflected in the churchwarden's book: "July 28, 1836 — To repairing the Church windows broken at the fair 10/-." And again on 26th July 1837: "To seeing after the Church at Dunwich fair, 2/-."

Dunwich, which had enjoyed the representation, by prescription and not by charter, of two Members in Parliament from the time of Edward I, was, in common with many other pocket boroughs, disfranchised in 1832, by which time the voters had shrunk to twelve in number, the last two members being Frederick Barne and the Earl of

Brecknock. However, it continued to be governed by bailiffs, aldermen and magistrates of its own choosing until the corporation was dissolved by the Municipal Corporation Act of 1883. The corporation property, including the appointment of trustees and the vestry, passed to the official trustees of charity lands.

Dunwich 'finds', have included Roman coins and some from William I onwards, a rare coin from the mint of King Stephen and a large percentage of cut-money, extremely interesting to numismatists. In one collection there was one quarter of William the Lion of Scotland; two pennies, three halves and six quarters of the first type issued by Henry II; larger types of Henry II and short-cross and long-cross coins. Then follow ten pennies, six half pennies and fifteen farthings of the first three Edwards, and one half-penny of Richard II most being of the London and Canterbury Mints.

Other finds include many miscellaneous objects of great interest, especially British enamelled work, the top of a crucifix bearing the Eagle of St John, pilgrims' tear-bottles, parts of pilgrims' pouches, cope hooks-and-eyes, shroud pins and clasps. Large spurs have also been found and many large and elaborate shoe buckles, one large thirteenth-century ring, and two bronze rings set with glass. Even mill stones have been found, the most interesting being those of coglomerate, quarried in Derbyshire. In a Mr Douce's collection, now at the Bodleian Library, are two posy rings found here, both of gold and inscribed. The first reads: "Let virtue be a guide to thee"; the second: "God alone made us two one".

There are one or two remarkable accounts of Dunwich, the first of which, attributed to the historian Stow, is contained in a letter written to John Day in 1573. It is now in the British Museum amongst the Harleian Manuscripts and is quoted in full by Suckling. The next account was made in 1589 by Radulph Agas, the eccentric and deformed cartographer who lived at Stoke by Nayland. It is to be found in Gardner's *History*.

The last account is contained in a chronological order of events as given by Gardner, in the seventeenth chapter of his work; much of the latter part of which is an eye-witness account:

The Church of Saint Felix and a Cell of Monks, were lost very early.

1286. On the Night after New-Years-Day, through the Vehemence of the Winds and Violence of the sea, several Churches were overthrown and destroyed in divers Places: Dunwich was one of the Sufferers.

The first Year of K. Edward III, the Old Port was rendered utterly useless.

Before the twenty-third Year of the said King, great Part of the Town and upwards of four hundred Houses which paid Rent to the Fee-Farm, with certain Shopes, and Windmills, were devoured by the sea.

The church of St Leonard overthrown.

In the fourteenth Century, the Churches of St Martin and St Nicholas were overthrown by the Waves of the Sea.

1385 Anno 8 Richard II. The Sea eat away the shore near the Black Friars.

1540 The Church of St John Baptist was taken down.

In that Century the Chapels of St Anthony, St Francis and St Katherine were overthrown.

Also South Gate and Gilden Gate, and not one Quarter of the Town left standing.

1570 Dunwich suffered incredible Damage.

1608 The High Road to the Sea was eaten away and another made through Peter Willet's Ground.

In the Reign of King Charles I, the Foundation of the Temple Buildings yielded to the irresistable Force of the undermining Surges.

1677 The Sea reached the Market Place, when the Townsmen sold the Lead of the Cross.

1680 All the Buildings North of Maison-Dieu-Lane were demolished.

1702 The Sea extended its Dominion to St Peter's Church, which was obliged to be broken down.

The Town Hall suffered the same fate.

1715 The Jail was undermined.

1729 The utmost Bounds of St Peter's Cemetery gave Place to the insulting Waves.

1740 Terrible Devastations were made in December. The Wind blowing very hard about North-East, with Continuance for several Days, occasioned great Seas, doing much Damage on the Coast during that Time by Inundations breaking down the Banks and overflowing many Marshes, &c. The sad effects thereof were severely felt by Dunwich, when a great Churchyard; and a great Road heretofore leading into the Town from the Key; leaving several naked Wells, Tokens of ancient Buildings. And from Maison Dieu Lane northwards, a continual Scene of Confusion. Part of the Old Key, built with stone, lay bare; making Canals cross the Beach, through which the River had Communications with the Sea, to the Hindrance of the People on Foot travelling that Way, for some Days. King's Holm, (alias Leonard's Marsh) heretofore valued at 200 and then at 100 Pounds per Annum, laid under Water and much Shingle and Sand thrown thereon from off the Beach; rendering it ever since of little worth; much of the Pasture and some of their arable Land, destroyed. The Sea raged with such Fury, that Cock and Hen Hills (which the preceding Summer were upwards of forty feet high, and in the Winter partly washed away) this Year, had their Heads levell'd with their bases, and the Ground about them so rent and torn, that the Foundation of St Francis's Chapel (which was laid between the said Hills) 'was discovered; where, besides the Ruins of the Walls, were five round Stones near of a Bigness; the Dimensions of one (I took) were four Feet the Diameter, and near two the Thickness. There was likewise a Circle of large Stumps of Piles, about twenty-four feet Circumference. The Bounds of the Cemetery were staked; within which the secret Repositories of the Dead were exposed to open View; several Skeletons, on the Ouze, divested of their Coverings; some lying in pretty good Order, others interrupted, and scattered, as the Surges carried them. Also a Stone Coffin, wherin were human bones covered with Tiles. Before a Conveniency offered for removing the Coffin, it was broke in two pieces (by the violence of the Sea) which serve now for Steps at each Foot of Deering Bridge.

At the same Time, and near the Chapel, the Pipes of an Aqueduct were found; some of Lead, others of gray Earth, like that of some urns. On the lowest part of the Chapel's Yard was the Flagg, retaining the old dead Grass; and in several Places, the Impression of the Spade; although it had been (beyond the Memory of the eldest Person in the Town) raised four or five Feet high with made Earth, bearing good Grass, Corn and Turnips; a Crop of the latter then growing thereon, but at that Time was reduced to Beach, over which the Sea plays ever since at high

Tides. Between that and Maison Dieu Lane many Roots of Trees were washed bare.

In November 1739, and some Time in the Winters 1746 and 1749, the Shingle and Sand were so abluted in some Places, by the Vehemence of the Furious waves of the Sea, which, at those Times, overflowed the Beach, that the Foundation of Houses, and the Banks, on each Side of the New Port, and Hummerston's Cut, were exhibited to open View.

In the Year 1740, as the Men of Dunwich were digging a Trench, near their Old Port, cross the Beach, to make a Watergang to drain their marshes and low Grounds, drowned the preceding Winter, by the Inundation of the Sea which drove prodigious Quantities of Shingle and Sand into the River, filling it in several Places, so that the Water could not disembogue itself they happened on a Stone Wall, cemented exceeding strong, which was part of their Old Key; and near that, on a Well; both which I saw as they were working. At which Time several Pieces of old Coins and other Curiosities were found . . .

And now this once famous Town or City, of a large Extent, the Buildings fair and many, well peopled, and wealthy; abounding with most Kinds of Merchandises, and the Source of Literature in those parts of the Kingdom; by the irresistable Impetuosity of the merciless sea, and the raging Plague of Fire, with which it hath been visited at sundry Times, is reduced to a narrow Compass; the Buildings few, and most of them mean; but one Church, some Remains of the Grey Friers, Saint James', and Maison Dieu Hospitals, and thirty-five Houses (including them in the Hospitals) are now standing, and about one hundred Souls subsisting; so that some of the Freemen, for Want of a sufficient Number, are obliged to serve or hold more Offices than one; and for the Generality, upon Account of the Stagnation of Trade, are poor and indigent. But the Inhabitants, by their Representatives erecting new Edifices, and repairing others, entertain reviving hopes of becoming once more a flourishing Town.

The chief Business carried on — at present, is the Fishery in the Bay, where are caught Herrings, Sprats, Soals, Flounders, Plaice, Cods, Haddocks, Whitings, Skeats, &c. whereby seven small Boats are occupied.

The great Alterations and Vicissitudes, of late Years, in several parts of Dunwich, are apparently conspicuous by Duck, alias Dukes Street; wherein at the latter End of Q. Ann's Reign, fourteen substantial Dwelling houses, besides Out houses, and Fish offices, were standing; all which are now utterly demolished, and a Bank cast up cross the West Entrance therein, where Middlegate stood, making it an Inclosure, which is now plowed, and the Face thereof so changed, that what was said of the once famous City, Troy, may be applied to this Street. *Jam Seges est ubi Troja fuit.*

A Platte of Dunwich was made by Christopher Saxton in 1575, who was a land surveyor in the employ of Thomas Seckford of Bealings. He was given to birds'-eye views. Ralph Agas is thought to have made one also, which is evidently referred to by Walpole in his *Anecdotes of Painting*: "Vertue had seen on a large skin of vellum a plan of the Town and boundaries of Dunwich in Suffolk, with its churches, adjacent villages, etc., and several remarks made by Radulphus Aggas in March 1589."

15

Men of Dunwich

It is only natural that in the course of the centuries Dunwich should have given birth to certain outstanding sons. A few have endured, but some there be whose names were writ in water. Of those remembered we might start with the Edgar family, of the Red House, Ipswich, who claimed descent from a John Edgar, of this city, which he left in A.D. 1237 and settled in North Glemham. They were granted a faculty pew in St Margaret's, Ipswich in 1695.

Members of the famous Wolsey family of East Suffolk, if they did not live in Dunwich, carried on the trades of butcher, combined, as was customary in those days, with that of innkeeper, at Yoxford, Dunwich, Blythburgh, Stowmarket, Ipswich and elsewhere. In 1405, a John Wulsy (the name is more often written Wulcy, which was the Cardinal's customary spelling), appears in the Court Rolls as holding land in Yoxford; and in 1410 his name appears again in the same rolls for Westwood Manor in Blythburgh. One peculiararity of the family is the frequent adoption of the christian name of John, so that John Wulcy becomes so numerous at times that they become designated John senior, John the middler and John junior. It is John Wulcy, the middler, whom is first found as holding a butcher's stall both at Dunwich and Blythburgh.

The best known of Dunwich sons was the subsequent Reformation Printer – John Deye, modernised to Day, born in the parish of St Peter's in 1522. He is first heard of in

London as practising his craft about 1544. He became one of the principal English publishers of his age, and the most practical typographer of his time, for he was the first English printer to use an Anglo-Saxon letter, and he introduced a new Italian letter.

Day secured the patronage of Archbishop Parker, which he found of use when, having obtained a lease to erect a shop in St Paul's Churchyard, and objections having been lodged by the Lord Mayor on behalf of his fellow book-sellers who were jealous of his monopoly, Day was able to call on him for aid. He prospered under Edward VI, and obtained a licence to print a catechism; but he was imprisoned under Mary. John Fox, the martyrologist, worked in Day's shop as a proof-reader, and three editions of the famous *Actes and Monuments of These Latter Perilous Dayes*, commonly known as the *Book of Martyrs*, were issued from his press. Day also produced one of the earliest almanacs, known as "a prognossicacion".

Day became a master of the reformed Stationer's Company in 1580, and on the occasion of Elizabeth he printed many of the theological treatises of the reformers. His trade mark represented a sleeper being awakened at dawn, with the caption — "Arise for it is Day," an allusion, not only to his name but to the Reformation. He was buried at Little Bradley, Suffolk, in 1584, where a brass was set up by his second wife, Alice le Hunt, who was also the mother of thirteen of his twenty-six children. His name today is commemorated in that of the John Day Publishing Company of New York.

Our next son brings us to the nineteenth century, when George Phillip (1804-92), an Oriental scholar, and third son of Francis Phillip, farmer, was born there on 11th January 1804; though he was baptised at Westleton, the adjoining parish, on 5th February. Francis Phillip, however, removed soon afterwards to Otley, where in 1887 George placed a clock in the church tower, to be known as the 'Phillip Clock', in remembrance of the early years of his life.

George Phillip first followed farming, but, after acquiring

a knowledge of mathematics, he became a master at the grammar school at Woodbridge, and from there he removed to Worcester. In 1824 he entered Magdalen Hall, Oxford, but after a short residence migrated to Queen's College, Cambridge on 25th October 1825, and matriculated. He graduated B.A. in 1829, M.A. in 1832, B.D. in 1839 and D.D. in 1859. In 1830 he was elected fellow of his college, and then took holy orders. He was presented by the college to the living of Sandon in Essex, where he remained until he was elected President of Queen's College. In 1861-2, Phillip was vice-chancellor, during which year the Prince of Wales was a student, and William Cavendish, seventh Duke of Devonshire, Chancellor.

Phillip worked at Oriental languages at a time when mathematics still held their supremacy at the university, and he met with slight encouragement. He taught Hebrew to the men of his own college and published a Syriac grammar in 1837, and an elaborate commentary on the Psalms in 1846. After his return to Cambridge he took a leading part in the establishment (in 1872) of the Indian-languages tripos and the Semitic-languages tripos. He was unwilling to accept the canons of the new criticism of the Old Testament. In 1887 he gave £1,000 to found a scholarship; and made a liberal donation towards building the new chapel in 1891. He died at Cambridge and his portrait was painted by Hubert Herkomer.

16

Ecclesiastical History of Dunwich

A good deal of legend and romance have grown up around the ecclesiastical history of Dunwich, which bear no relation to historic fact. It is quite evident that fifty-two churches never existed there, even allowing that some may have disappeared before the making of Domesday, or that that record is not strictly correct. The story too, of the 'Golden Gates', as also that of the mint, belongs to the pretty legends of steeples seen below water, or the sound of bells coming out of the tide. However, it is only natural such tales should run, and it is but a commentary on the greatness that was Dunwich.

As we have seen, only one church existed at the time of the Confessor, although two more sprang up between then and Domesday; and as the encroachment of the sea was a continuous process, it is probable that not all the parish churches existed at one and the same time. Apart from that of St Felix (if it ever existed), it is known that six parish churches went to the making of the city: St Leonard's, St Peter's, St John's, St Martin's, St Nicholas's, and last and, as some would have it, least, All Saints' of modern memory. Some of these were undoubtedly fine buildings, some cruciform with central towers; but it must not be concluded that all had reached maturity, as some were probably in the embryo stage of nave and chancel. Even so, if all were not fully developed, it is also equally certain that none were in that state of decay and neglect which fell on so many of our parish churches in later years; and some must have gone over the cliff in all their glory.

155

It is interesting to note, and there may be foundation for thinking, that Felix taught the Anglo-Saxons the use of flint in the building of churches, which has so greatly influenced the external decoration of our splendid East Anglian heritage. If such was the case, the flints would have been provided by the then existent industry, which has been carried on 'years out of mind' at Brandon.

Imagination can picture this Dunwich with its religious buildings, almost all branches of which seem to have been represented. There may have been one or two round towers, such as those at Frostenden, Thorington and Bramfield, marking the meanderings of the Dunwich river; memorials of ancient days and ancient dreads. Some were guild churches, for a *Gildae Mercatorias* was established here under King John, and there were also the 'Gild of St John,' 'Gild of Our Lady' (mentioned 1521), 'Gild of the Holy Name of Jesus' (mentioned 1525), 'Gild of St Katherine' and 'Gild of Brethren of the Chapel'. Certainly all contained, in greater or lesser degree, the craftsmanship of the medieval workman, later to attract the attention of Mr William Dowsing, who from despised All Saints took down thirty pictures and twenty-eight cherubims.

A writer in *Archaeologica* has commented on the peculiar character of the development of the parish church in these districts. Elsewhere in England the churches apparently had been built, and held by thanes and large landowners, but in East Anglia they were frequently on the land of groups of freemen and others, by whom, or by whose predecessors, they were probably built and endowed. This 'communal' action in the building of churches is not to be found in any other part of England.

It must be borne in mind also how great a part these parish churches formed in the civic life of the town, contributing to the social welfare with their manor courts, church ales, plays, bakehouses, feats; even markets, sometimes inside the church, certainly common in the churchyards. To say nothing about the parish water supply, forge

and breweries, controlled directly or indirectly by the
church; and above all the right of sanctuary. They provided
too, officers for the locality, for the present town clerks
are in direct lineal descent from the parish clerks; while the
church wardens were the custodians of all kinds of private
treasures, and even acted as pawnbrokers and money-
lenders of church property and wealth. When the townsman
made his almost daily visit to his church to say a prayer
before his favourite saint, or visited the chapel of St
Nicholas to request the protection of that saint for a safe
voyage of his vessel bound for Iceland, he would tread on
ground most holy, and behold things most sacred in the
eyes of a devout worshipper. It is also certain that somewhere in these numerous churches, would be found an altar
to St Eloi, the first Apostle of Christianity in Flanders,
since the Flemings made of Dunwich a home.

Dunwich remained a see for some two hundred years,
Felix being succeeded first by his deacon, Thomas, and
then by Boniface. He in turn was succeeded by Bisus, also
written Bosa, who was consecrated in 669. This prelate
split the diocese in two, establishing another see at North
Elmham, he remaining at Dunwich. Acca or Etta came
next, then followed Astwolf and Eadferth, consecrated in
734. Next came Cuthwin, Alberth, Eglaf, Headred and
Alsin or Aelfun, who is reputed to have been buried in
Dunwhich, *vide* the *Anglo-Saxon Chronicle* for 799: "This
year Bishop Alfin died at Sudbury and was buried at
Dunwich, and Tidfrith was consecrated after him." Were-
mund succeeded Tidfrith, and then followed Wybred, who
was the last bishop of the independent see of Dunwich as
he reunited the two sees about 870 and removed it to
Elmham.

For a time the Danish invasion extinguished both
bishoprics, until Elmham was re-established about 960, and
remained so until the first year of William the Conqueror,
when Harfustus, the twenty-third biship, changed its seat to
Thetford, where it remained until the time of William

Rufus. It was then changed by the licence of that monarch to Norwich. The bishopric of Dunwich has been revived in name in later years, as a title given to a suffragan of St Edmundsbury and Ipswich, instituted in 1934.

From the time of Wybred, Dunwich sank to the status of a rural deanery, under the Archdeacon of Suffolk, which in 1246 was divided into thirteen deaneries, the deanery of Dunwich having forty-eight parishes.

Mention must be made too, of the builders of these Dunwich churches, as to whether they were local craftsmen or masons imported from Flanders. Certainly there were local men, for one Richard Russell of Dunwich, with others, contracted for the building of Walberswick steeple in 1426. In any case their materials for the stone dressings must have littered the wharves of the old port, brought thither in those crazy craft from Caen and elsewhere. And we can be thankful there still remains the delightful evidence of their work in the two Franciscan gateways, as also in the lazar chapel by the modern church.

In addition to the parish churches already mentioned, there were three chapels — those of St Anthony, St Francis and St Catherine — and two hospitals — those of St James and Holy Trinity, or Maison Dieu. Added to which was the parish of Minsmere, situated a quarter of a mile from Minemere Haven. To these must be added the Temple Church of the Knights Templars, and the two great religious orders of St Francis and St Dominic, the Grey and Black Friars.

St Leonard's was a vicarage and is mentioned as early as 1065. It was appropriated to the Priory of Eyé. Gardner thought it stood east of St John, and that it was early lost, circa 1340 to 1400.

One Richard was a priest of this parish, and Roger Crystepen gave a piece of land, situated here, to the Prior and Convent of Eye, for the good of his soul; the deed of which is dated Friday, Feast of St Hilary, 1270. In a will dated 1540, a testator devised his house in the parish, anciently called St Leonard.

St John Baptist, a rectory, was evidently a noble build-ing — cruciform, with a central tower — and stood by the great market place in the centre of the town. In 1510, in an effort to save it from destruction, a jetty was built in front to arrest the inroads of the sea. The last institution was in 1537, and three years later it was pulled down. In the chancel was discovered a large gravestone, under which was unearthed a stone coffin that contained the body of a man in a perfect state of preservation. He was wearing pointed shoes, known as crakows, imported into this country from Krakov, while on his breast were two chalices of a coarse metal. This gave rise to the speculation that he was one of the Bishops of Dunwich, possibly Alsin or Aelfun. As the disturbers gazed on the dead, the corpse resolved into dust.

This was a guild church, for here were the Guilds of St John Baptist and St Katherine, and in the north aisle was a chapel dedicated to St Nicholas. In 1542, the church-wardens sold plate to the value of £21, "which was bestowed in making a pere for the defence of the churche and thole town". In 1544 another £17 was realised and used in like manner.

St Peter's was a rectory and is reputed to have stood sixty rods north-east of All Saints. It was adorned with a cross on the top of the steeple, which Mr Dowsing duly removed, together with sixty-three cherubims, sixty Jesus's in capital letters on the roof and forty 'pictures' (stained-glass windows). John Day, the printer was a native of this parish, as we have seen. He is reported to have made a gift of an image to be set up in the church, but as he was a Reformer it was probably a book, which may have been the famous *Book of Martyrs*.

Again this was a guild church, with a Jesus Guild, for in 1525 one Robert King in his testament stated: "I will and do give to Jesus Gild, £3. 13. 4d." It was evidently one of the last churches to disappear, for Gardner states that the churchyard was swallowed up by the sea "not more than twenty years ago", when the last remains of the dead were sticking out of the cliff. A long list of persons who desired to be buried there testifies to its influence and importance.

About the year 1413, a carpenter, one John of Eye, when repairing the roof of the chancel, fell off the scaffolding and was killed.

In 1597 after Bishop Redman's visitation of the Norwich diocese, Robert Watkinson, curate of Dunwich, was presented and admonished, or so it was alleged, because he "practizeth physicks". He was curate of this church. (*The Country Priest in English History*, by H. Tindal Hart.)

A memo dated 1698 states that the chancel end fell on 11th December 1688, and in 1697, half the steeple fell down the cliff; and the last service was held about 1654. The church was taken down in 1702.

The register of this church, missing like so many others, was located at the British Museum by the late Charles Partridge, a scholarly local historian. It now forms Add MSS 3/561, and on the fly-leaf is inscribed:

A Regester booke of all the marriages crysteninges and burialls that hath been in the parishe of St Peters in dunwich within the countie of Suff. Since the yere of our Lord God. 1539.
Memorandum.   March 11, 1698
  Mr Tho Rosse, vicar of Westleton gave me this old Registerbook belonging to ye Church of St Peter's Dunwich, a spacious fine old church now devoured by ye Sea, ye chancelles end falling upon ye 11 of December, Anno 1688, and in ye winter 1697 halfe of ye steeple fell down ye Cliffe, so yt ye sea in 9 years space gott that church wch was near as long as Blyburgh. I have been often (in) itt but never before ye roofe and windows were down and all ye gravestones gone. Mr Brown, 20 years Vicar of Wenhaston, was ye last yt preached in or about ye (year) 1654 or 55, as Mr Driver a very ancient inhabitant there living to about 80 years of age has very often told me, and yt ye church was curiously glazed with painted glass quite thro' and many gravestones with inscriptions upon brass, with 4 bells wch he said he help to remove to All Saints Church ye only church now in use.
  This was written by Thos Leman Esq, of Wenhaston, J. Leman.

St Martin's also was a rectory, and is thought to have

stood on the east side of the town. The Prior of Eye was a patron and the last institution was in 1335, which suggest an early loss. In the Taxatio of Edward III, a hundred houses were in this parish, but by 1342 only seven remained, and no chaplain would serve the altar, as there were no gifts. It is mentioned as early as 1291 and disappeared between 1340 and 1360.

St Nicholas was evidently another fine church and is first mentioned in 1150. It was another of the cruciform churches, with a central tower and a rectory, and is supposed to have stood twenty rods south-east of Black Friars. Moreover, it was the largest of the parish churches in the town. The last institution was made in 1382, soon after which it was devoured by the sea. An interesting item relative to this church, was a stone taken from its walls, which served as a keystone to a window of a house in Dunwich for many years. It was inscribed¹ "*Sce Nicholas ora pro nobis.*" The Prior of Eye was a patron and the church paid one mark yearly to two synods.

All Saints was the last of the Dunwich parish churches to disappear, and its crumbling ruins on the cliff familiarised generations of Dunwich lovers with the ancient town. It is not too much to say that the ruins of All Saints was Dunwich to the world at large. Gardner speaks of it as being "esteemed but mean", and then goes on to describe what must have been, at one time, an extremely rich and beautiful church. If, therefore, its 'meanness' was comparative, then its fellows that departed earlier, must have been noble. It was a vicarage, and appropriated to the convent of Eye, and is thought to have been begun about 1350. Either it was rebuilt about 1527, or a new aisle was added at that time, for it consisted of a nave, a north aisle, separated from the nave by octagon shafts, a chancel and a square tower, which at one time rejoiced in a clock and three bells. The first or little bell was cast in 1725, the second in 1678 and the third in 1626. As already mentioned, Mr Dowsing visited here, removed thirty superstitious pictures, twenty-eight cherubim and a cross on the chancel.

Gardner goes on to say that in the north aisle, were "magisterial seats decorated with curious carved work, resembling those in Southwold church; while the windows were adorned with painted glass, which the glaziers, without regard to it or the founder, brake in pieces. This aisle was pulled down in 1725 and gravestone, taken from the floor, were used to block up the arches. Most of the gravestones had plates of brass with inscriptions to the memory of persons buried there; all which were embezzled when the aisle was pulled down. On some of the gravestones (as I have heard the masons report) were grooves, wherein were inscriptions unintelligible to any of them: and that they were all laid for the foundation of the new wall in 1725, when the aisle was taken down by faculty: and the lead, with other materials was sold by John Shipman and Francis Swatman church wardens to repair the remains of the church." The following measurements of the church are given: nave 91 feet by 22 feet, chancel 40 feet by 21 feet, tower 16 feet by 10 feet, giving a total length of 147 feet.

A memorial that adorned this church was stolen, but was happily restored, in part, by the Norwich Corporation, and is now in the succeeding parish church of St James. It is a brass plate bearing the figures of a man, 'Jone' his wife, a son, Michael, and six daughters; with the following inscription:

Here Thomas Cooper sutym baly of this town, inclosed is in clay,
Which is the resting place of flesh, until the latter day.
Of one sonne and daughters six, the Lord hym parent made,
Ere cruel death did work his spight, or fickle life did fade.
Who deceased the XVII of Maye, in the year of our Lord 1576.

By his will this Thomas Cooper gave £5 to the town of Dunwich to be paid unto the use of the key of the town.

It appears that, owing to the publicity given to the restoration and the unveiling of this memorial in April 1928, a copy of Gardner's book was produced that contained the original letter from the man who stole the brass. He was Daniel Bonhote, an attorney, or clerk, to Henry Negus, attorney of Harleston. Negus was also town clerk of Dunwich 1764-82.

On 29th August 1770 a grand assembly was held at Dunwich, Henry Negus, town clerk, being present, with his clerk. The letter, dated Bungay, 31st August 1770, speaks of the ruinous condition of the church, after scraping a stone with his boot, he adds: 'At last I spyed the brasses which I send herewith. The first sight of them inspired me (if the sight of a piece of brass ever inspired anyone) with a friendly joy, and I immediately set to work about getting them up, and with only one person with me, who by putting a plum in his hand to enjoin him to secrecy, assisted me, and soon effected it. This piece of theft, if discovered, may you know, subject me to some inconveniences though I don't say it is anyways likely. However, I must look to you to indeminifye me against the consequences. The resemblance of the girls to the mother, and the boy to the father, seems to me a master-piece, and the perfection of the whole will, I hope, make it an acceptable addition to your cabinet." The letter was addressed to a Mr Toos, no address.

The lands appertaining to this church in Gardner's time, were about £4 per annum. He proceeds further: "All Saints is the only one in being where divine service is celebrated from Lady Day to Michaelmas, once a fortnight and monthly the succeeding half year; the minister's stipend not exceeding twelve pounds by the year, exclusive of a small provisional allowance for refreshment, in consideration of his journey thither. The church is esteemed but mean, and built with flint and freestone, which old age has reduced to a tottering state, especially the chancel. The inside walls, too, are infected with an incurable spreading leprosy; yet it still retains some grandeur by the roof, and antiquity of the graven stones, which are wide at head and narrow at feet. The tower, built of flint and freestone, with various decorations, is old but pretty strong, and indifferently handsome; crowned with a battlement, each angle supporting an angel, representing Gabriel, Michael, Raphael and Uriel; whereof one is blown down and destroyed."

The last service of All Saints was held about 1755; the east end disappeared over the cliff in February 1904, and the steeple on 12th November 1919. The last remaining buttress of the tower, which remained on the cliff like a warning finger, was taken down and has been re-erected in the churchyard of St James. Even there it had a narrow escape when a German bomb fell just behind it, but did no damage. The lead from the roof was sold for £124 15s. 6d, and three old bells for £70 8s. 0d.

Davy, the local historian, was at Dunwich on 24th October 1839 and reported that the steeple appeared to be in tolerable repair (indeed it was kept in repair by Trinity House for a long time, as a landmark for ships; and a blacksmith from Westleton put an iron band round it, a difficult feat), and that he remembered a man named Parker, who had occupied a farm at Yoxford, being convicted and transported for stealing one of the bells and some lead.

St James was erected in 1830, largely through the instrumentality of Michael Barne, who had represented Dunwich in four Parliaments. It was built in the grounds of the lazar hospital of that name. Mr Bird of Yoxford, left it on record that when the foundations were dug, a very large quantity of human skeletons was unearthed, that had been buried without much attention to order. Evidently these were the remains of the lepers, inmates of the hospital. The earliest register of the church dates from 1672, which had been removed here from All Saints.

Gardner quotes a statement that the Register of Eye mentions that the churches of St Michael and St Bartholomew were swallowed by the sea before the year 1331, when the prior and convent of Eye petitioned the Bishop of Norwich to impropriate the church of Laxfield to them; and amongst other reasons for it, alleged that they lost a considerable part of their revenues at Dunwich by the breaking in of the sea. But he could find no other reference or trace of these. Both of the above mentioned churches are referred to in 1086, but seem to have disappeared by 1287.

Convent of Franciscan Friars or Friars Minor is perhaps the most interesting of all the ecclesiastical institutions of Dunwich, with its continuous grey and lichened walls, almost intact; and the two gateways, beautiful still in their decay, expressing work well done and finely conceived. The larger gate served as the principal entrance to the house and one can see again the magnificent retinue of some traveller passing through (welcome or otherwise) as the great gates open. The lesser gate served for the ordinary folk, going to and from the chapel. There was evidently another gate in the east wall, which has been closed up.

A good deal of speculation has run as to what might lie under the turf inside those walls, and some archaeological work has been carried on there in recent years. This, however, has not yielded anything of great interest beyond unearthing the foundations of the former buildings. The ruins within the walls have served various purposes since the Dissolution, one part being a residence, another as a hall for the business of the corporation, and at another time the jail was housed there. What alterations and additions these various uses involved were eventually cleared away and the ruins left intact.

The convent was founded, circa 1265, by Richard Fitz-John and Alice his wife, and augmented by Henry III. The site was either changed or added to during the reign of Edward I, who issued a writ of enquiry in 1289 to determine whether the proposed alteration would be pre-judicial to his interest or no. Having been informed by the escheater that it would not be to his disadvantage, a grant in mortmain was made 25th August 1290 for part of the King's Dyke to be enclosed and built over by the friars, who thus, by permission of the Corporation of Dunwich, breached its ancient fortifications; the area involved being four and a half acres, sixteen perches.

The following entry in the Patent Rolls, would seem to confirm that the present site is not the original one: "1328, October 23, Salisbury. Licence for the Friars Minor of Dunwich to enclose and hold the vacant plot there, of the yearly value of 2/-, which they used to inhabit, and which was taken into the King's hands because they removed to another place in the town, as it would be indecent that a plot of ground for some time dedicate to divine worship, where christian bodies are buried, should be converted to human uses". Further precautions to preserve this site were taken in 1415.

The heart of Dame Hawise Poynings was buried here, and Gardner recalls an interesting incident. A workman in removing a mole that stood within the walls of the monastery, discovered a brass buckle which lay on top of a small earthenware vessel, which he broke in pieces thinking it contained treasure. On this urn was inscribed, *Ave Maria, gracia plena*, and it was conjectured that it might have contained the heart in question. The times were reflected in the following: "This man being a servant durst not neglect his master's time to make diligent search, although he was inclined to think there were more things."

Several seals of this house have been preserved, and in 1754, when an old house was taken down in Dunwich, another seal was found. The pointed oval fifteenth century Seal of the Franciscan Friars of Dunwich bears St John Baptist under a canopied arch with nimbus, clothed in a camel skin, its head hanging at his feet, holding in the left hand the Agnus Dei on a plaque, and pointing to it with the right hand. By the side of the Baptist is a kneeling friar, with a scroll, bearing: "S:Joh:Ora:P': me". The legend is: "SIGILLU:GARDIANI:MINOR:DONEWYCY."

Gardner gives a reproduction of another remarkable seal of this friary, representing a ship with a large mainsail; at the bow is seated a crowned king, and at the stern a mitred bishop with crozier in left hand. The legend is: "SIGILLU': FR'M:MINOR:DONEWIC."

The order of Dominican or Black Friars, instituted in 1206 by St Dominic, came to England in 1221, and to Dunwich soon after. It was so named from the colour of the cloaks worn. The monastery was founded there in 1256, by Sir Roger de Holishe, who was subsequently buried in the church. This was situated in the parish of St John, 120 rods distant from Grey Friars, probably eastwards as it was nearly destroyed before 1384. Building of a considerable nature was going on in the thirteenth century, because on 9th April 1256 Henry III, gave these friars seven oaks for timber, out of any of the royal forests of Essex.

As in the case of the Grey Friars, an addition was made to the Black Friars' grounds in 1349; on 12th October the King licenced John de Wengefield to assign five acres to them for the enlargement of their site. Incursions of the sea were evidently troubling them in 1384, when they sought powers, through Robert de Swillington, to "acquire 10 acres of land and four of marsh at Blythburgh, held in chief for building them a new mansion house, there to remove." But this was never done and they remained in Dunwich until the Dissolution. The churchyard of St Nicholas became part of their grounds when the church fell into decay, about 1413.

A letter written to Thomas Cromwell in November 1538 by the ex-prior of this house, who had been made a suffragan bishop of Dover, informed him that he had suppressed twenty houses of friars, amongst them being the Black and Grey of Dunwich. The lead from these despoiled houses lay near the water, and was therefore ready to be taken to London, or elsewhere.

St James's Hospital was situated without the gates, and very wealthy. It is mentioned as early as 1189. This was an institution for the alleviation of leprosy, and consisted of a master and leprous brothers, and later, sisters; it was a wealthy foundation until unscrupulous masters wasted the revenues and reduced it to a sad condition. The church was considered to have been a fine building, consisting of a nave, chancel and sanctum-sanctorum, the entire length of which is given as 107 feet 7 inches. Blomefield, the Norfolk historian, thought John, Earl of Moreton, afterwards King of England, was the founder; while others have credited Walter de Riboff, though probably he was the principal benefactor. "The church is a great one," wrote Weaver, "and a fair large one of the old fashion, and divers tenements, houses, and lands to the same belonging, to the use of the poor, sick and impotent people there."

On 30th January 1744, an interesting discovery was made in the sanctum-sanctorum, when a repository of relics belonging to the church was unearthed, and nearby a portrait of a man, presumably St James. These had probably been concealed at the Reformation. The portrait remained there until divine services ceased, which was about the time of Charles II, when the church fell into decay and everything was destroyed. The revenue was made from land at Heveningham, Brandeston, Dunwich and Carlton Colville. This was used as a salary of 40s. per annum for the master, and the residue applied to the maintenance of three or four people, who resided in an adjacent delapidated house, the sole survivor of their once-wealthy establishment. The Hospital disappeared after 1640.

The thirteenth-century seal shows a full-length figure of St James, with nimbus, having the right-hand raised in benediction and a crutch or cross-tau in the left. On each side is an escallop shell. The legend is: "SIGILL':SACTI: JACOBI:I .. DON.".

The Holy Well of St James is, or was, in a field west of the hospital. The water came from a spring running through a gravel bed, and when analysed was found to contain chlorine, sulphuric acid, silica, lime and magnesia. This may have been a place of pilgrimage for those afflicted with ophthalmic troubles, and may have supplied the inmates of the hospital with water. It was used in later years by the local women for washing their linen, as the water was extremely soft and sparkling.

Maison Dieu or Holy Trinity was a house of great priviliges, and founded in very early years. It first appears in the records in the time of Henry III, circa 1250, and may have been founded by that monarch. It consisted of a master and six brethren, sisters appearing later. Some of the masters were of repute, one being an esquire, another an M.A.; but in time evil men came to its rule and the like fate befell it to that of St James. Weaver writing of it says: "The which Maison Dieu was an house of great privilege, and a place exempt, and there was a very little proper house, and a proper lodging for the Master of the same, for the time being to dwell in."

There was a church for the use of poor people thereto belonging, which appears to have been rebuilt or repaired about 1527. Amongst the treasures here preserved was a cross of great sanctity, which was not only coveted but stolen by the Abbot of St Osyth, who, however, was compelled to restore it to Adam de Brom, then master.

The revenue in Gardner's time had dwindled to £11 17s., which was made up from land at "Ellow, Blithford, Dunwich". Out of this came the master's salary of £2 a year the remainder being divided as at St James. Later, the two hospital revenues were combined for the poor people in Dunwich, passing to the jurisdiction of the trustees under the Charity Commissioners.

A chapel in Dunwich, called God's House, has been void and without a warden for 2¼ years, and the goods belonging thereto are not sufficient for the maintenance of the five brethren dwelling there.

The gift of the said chapel belongs to the king, and six brethren have been wont to dwell there of whom one is dead: the brethren have received the Issues in the time of voidence for their maintenance, and have spent them in good uses.

This hospital and church disappeared after 1640.

The Maison Dieu has been happily commemorated by the Town Trust, who erected in 1931 two almshouses, which bear a tablet to that effect, inscribed with the ancient seal of the hospital. The common seal of this house is a large oval, bearing in the centre the three lions of Henry III, surmounted by a triple cross, on the lowest limb of which are two fleurs-des-les. The legend is: "SIGILLUM. FRATRUM.DOMUS.DEI.DONEWICO."

The Temple or Preceptory of Knights Templars was described by Gardner as "a very old church, vaulted over and the aisle leaded". It stood near Middle Gate Street, having Duck Street on the north and Covent Garden on the south, and was about forty-five rods distant from All Saints. It was endowed with great privileges for pardon, and owned considerable property, houses, rents and lands, both free and copyhold, in Westleton, Dingle and Dunwich; including a windmill given it by John de Cove in 1185, and a manor with a fee farm rent of 16s. 6d., which extended to Westleton and Middleton. The Dunwich Temple Court, for gathering and collecting its revenues, was held on All Saints Day, 2nd November. The church was dedicated to the Virgin Mary and St John Baptist, and styled in wills, the "Temple of Our Lady in Dunwich" and once as *Hospitale beate Marie et s. Johannis vocat le Tempil*. It flourished until the Dissolution of the order in 1540. The Temple Manor eventually came to the Barne family and consisted of "two acres near a house abutting on the town ditch and cliff".

King John confirmed to the order their lands and other liberties, and in 1252 the *"bona Templariorum de Done-wico"* were valued at 11s. a year. The Temple first belonged to the Knights Templars, a religious and military order which was founded in 1117, and became the richest in the world. Their first house was erected on the site of Solomon's Temple, hence their designation. It was suppressed in England in 1312, by Edward II.

The order was succeeded by the Hospitallers, who had a very good estate in Dunwich, and it is probable they kept their church for the use of their own tenants, whose houses all bore crosses, the badge of the knights. Adhering in England and Ireland to the bishop of Rome against Henry VIII, the order was suppressed, and the lands and goods referred to the King's disposition. Mary replaced the order, but Elizabeth I finally dissolved it, and granted its possessions in Dunwich to a Thomas Andrews, 12th February 1562, as parcel of the Possessions of the Preceptors of Battisford. James I, on 13th August 1623, granted it to Ellis Rothwell, who gave it to Millicent his wife, who after his death sold it to Thomas Knivett of Ashwelthorpe (who died 3rd December 1629). Sir John Rous of Henham Hall married as his second wife, Elizabeth, daughter of Thomas Knivett, by whom the manor descended to her grandson, John Rous. He sold it to Charles Long, who disposed of it to Miles Barne.

The present Lovers' Lane was the old Middlegate Street, and ran just south of the Temple Mound, then bent northwards into the heart of the city. Excavations carried out on this Temple Hill in 1935 revealed little or nothing. This was so named from being in close proximity to the Knights Templars, which stood south of Middlegate Street. It was in reality a look-out post, or possibly a beacon mound, connected with the defences of the city, or even the defences of the country itself. There is another such mound at Walberswick and another at Leiston.

Dunwich Temple Mound stood hard by the 'Pales Dyke' which was an earthen bank or rampart surmounted by a palisade that ran from the sea at Minsmere, where it was gated, to the King's Flue or river, and formed the defences of the city on the land side. In March 1752 its extent was

133 poles, 13 feet. "Old inhabitants remembered it with a hedge and large trees on top."

Phillip and Mary made a grant of rents and lands in Dunwich, to the Hospital of St John of Jerusalem, to the restoration of the order, which they accomplished, and which was revived by them into that of St John of Clerkynwell. (This might well have been the property originally belonging to this Order in Dunwich.) Calendar of Patent Rolls.

The foundations of the Knights Templars disappeared in the reign of James I. Curiously enough, it was the Arms of the Templars that provided the Dunwich Arms, viz: "Gu.a cross Argent".

We now come to three chapels — St Anthony, St Francis, St Katherine. St Anthony was swallowed by the sea at a very early date. It is not known where it stood. St Francis stood between Cock and Hen Hills, and was suppressed in 1545. A lease of the house and meadow was granted to George Waller in 1595 for fifty-five years at 20s. a year payable to the use of St Peter's parish. St Katherine stood in the parish of St John and was suppressed like St Francis. There was a guild belonging to the chapel.

The Common Garden or Cell of the Priory of Eye, probably of the Order of St Benedict, is mentioned by M.R. James as being here. Common or Convent Garden, abutting on Sea Fields, was a plot of ground whereon grew large crops of thyme etc., which created in many people a belief that it was a garden for the service of the whole town. But the name rather imports the foundation of some convent thereabouts. Also mention is made of a cell of monks at Dunwich subordinate to Eye, "destroyed some ages past", so probably it was a curtilage appertaining to this religious house. "And as the sea made encroachment thereon many human bones were discovered, whereby part therof manifestly appeared to have been a place of sepulture, which was washed away in the winter of 1740". Leland states that the monks of Eye, in his time, possessed an ancient textus, or book of the Gospels, brought from this Cell, called in later days 'The Red Book of Eye', and which had belonged to Felix.

Almshouses existing in Dunwich were all destroyed before Gardner's time. He also records the generosity of a gentleman who allowed "£20, a year for a master to instruct and educate the poor children of the town, but which bounty was witholden, and the place has felt lamentable want of learning for more than 20 years past."

In addition to the foregoing list of churches, Claude Morley in his *Check List*, gives St Peter Priory, probably founded in Saxon days and mentioned in the *Feet of Fines*, which disappeared about 1307. He also gives St Mary Chapel, mentioned 1340 in the *Nonarum*.

We might end this survey of Dunwich with lines written by Agnes Strickland,, of *Queens of England* fame:

> Oft gazing on thy craggy brow,
>   We muse on glories o'er;
> Fair Dunwich! thou art lowly now,
>   Renown'd and sought no more.
>
> How proudly rose thy crested seat
>   Above the ocean wave;
> Yet doom'd beneath that sea to meet
>   One wide and sweeping grave!
>
> The stately city greets no more
>   The home-returning bark;
> Sad relics of her splendours o'er
>   One crumbling spire we mark.
>
> Unlike when ruled by Saxon powers,
>   She sat in ancient pride,
> With all her stately halls and towers
>   Reflected on the tide.
>
> Those who through each forgotten age
>   With patient care will look,
> Will find her fate in many a page
>   Of Time's extended book.

SELECT BIBLIOGRAPHY

Gardner's *Dunwich*, published 1754.
Suckling, *History of Suffolk.*
East Anglian Miscellany.
Proceedings of the Suffolk Institute of Archaeology.
Victoria County History.
J. Reid Moir, *The Antiquity of Man in East Anglia*, 1927.
H.C. Darby, *Domesday Geography of East Anglia.*
Dictionary of National Biography, 1896.
Oxford Dictionary of English Place Names, 1936.
W.W. Skeat, *The Place-Names of Suffolk*, 1913.
G.N. Garmonsway, *The Anglo-Saxon Chronicle*, 1953.
M.R. James, *Suffolk and Norfolk*, 1930.
The Domesday Book. Translated by Lord J.W.N. Hervey.
R. Rainbird Clarke, *East Anglia.* 1960.

17

Southwold and the Battle of Sole Bay

In this country [England] it is thought well to kill an admiral from time to time to encourage the others. Voltaire.

It is difficult to associate the peaceful little town of Southwold with wars and rumours of wars. Yet it was the centre-piece of the third Dutch War, fought between ourselves, with the French, and the Dutch for the supremacy of the sea on Whit-Monday, 28th May 1672.

Before that great day the town had seen much coming and going of sick and wounded seamen, because there had been sporadic fighting up and down the coast prior to this engagement. There was a fight off Lowestoft on the 3rd June 1665. This was described as a most signal victory for the English and the severest blow the Dutch ever felt at sea.

One of Southwold's proud survivals after the town had been ravaged by two disastrous fires is the present Sutherland House, which local tradition has identified as being the headquarters of James, Duke of York, Lord High Admiral of the Fleet and the commander of the Red in the famous battle.

In 1664 the King's Council commissioned the magistrates of the town to be ready to accommodate and tend the sick and wounded that might be landed from any of His Majesty's ships; also "to fitt Places of Security to keep such Prisoners as shall be sent".

The combined fleet of England and France consisted of 101 sail of men-of-war, besides fire ships and tenders, carrying 6,018 guns and 34,500 men. The Dutch mustered 168 sail, including fire ships and tenders, 91 of which were men-of-war. The commanders of the combined squadron were James, Duke of York (the Red), Count D'Etrees (the White), and the earl of Sandwich (the Blue). Against these were De Ruyter, Blankart and Van Ghent; with Cornelius De Witt as deputy from the states.

There is a very good description of the Battle in Wake's *Southwold*, as also in Gardner's *Dunwich*. The English and French lay upon the bay in a very negligent manner. Sandwich warned his brother commanders of their danger, but the Duke of York considered this to be a reflection on his courage. However, when the enemy bore down on them many of the ships had to cut their cables in order to get into action. Sandwich left room for his comrades to disengage themselves by hastening out of the bay. If he had not done so, the fire ships of the enemy would have destroyed our ships.

It was now Sandwich's turn to show he was no coward. It is recorded that he was at every point of danger. He encountered the entire squadron of Van Ghent's single-handed, killed the Dutch admiral with his own hand, sinking a man-of-war and three other enemy vessels. At this moment his battered ship, the *Royal James*, was grappled and fired. Of the thousand men who formed the crew but few escaped. His officers were all cut down, himself surrounded by flames, but he was advised to seek safety – in vain. At the end he flung himself into the sea; it was thought largely because of the stupid aspersion on his bravery.

In the meantime the Duke of York was hotly pressed by De Ruyter, so much so, that, of the thirty-two actions in which he had been previously engaged, he declared this to be the hottest. His ship, the *Prince*, disabled, he moved his flag to the *St Michael*; and a third time to the *London*. Darkness brought the engagement to a close, in which the losses on both sides were heavy but about equal. The casualties sustained by the Dutch were never published.

The only ship lost by us was the *Royal James*, but the

loss of commanders was heavy, including "several lieutenants and inferior officers, whose names it were too tedious a business to set down". Our forces captured one man-of-war, the *Stevern*, of forty-eight guns and another of fifty-two guns, the *Joshua*, which became leaky and was sunk. Two others were also sunk, one by the Earl of Sandwich, the other by Sir Edward Spragg.

Wake ends his account with a nice little tribute to the Southwolders, who were anxiously watching on shore, but were prevented by a thick fog from beholding events. "But the unceasingly-ascending smoke, the constant roaring of the guns, and the quickly-repeated concussions, which shook them in their houses and standing-places, held them, as it were, spell-bound by excitement and panic. Under these impressions they were induced, as the day advanced, to muster a strong guard that, in case of a defeat by sea, Southwold might be prepared to give a warm reception to the enemy on shore. From a similar feeling, they prevented the country people who had flocked into the town to behold the fight from repassing the bridge, before victory was decided in favour of England."

On 10th June a ketch sweeping for anchors on the Sunk sand, happened on the body of the Earl of Sandwich. He was wearing his George, Star and Garter, and three diamond rings. The body was taken to Landguard Fort where it was embalmed and lay in state in the chapel until it was removed to London, where it was buried in Henry VII's chapel in Westminster Abbey.

His face was crushed, but no sign of burning was upon him. Sir Charles Lyttleton wrote: "He was a wonderful fat man. There was not a pint of water run from him, but his being so mightily swelled proceeded rather from wind than water." It was supposed therefore, that he died from shock caused by jumping into the water from a great height, as he was neither burnt nor drowned.

White in his Eastern England states that the sound of the firing during the battle was heard far inland. The Earl of Ossory, who commanded the *Victory*, was on a visit to Euston Hall. He immediately took horse and galloped off to join his ship. It might also be mentioned that as the action took place at Whitsuntide, many of the offiers and men were on land merrymaking, and never got back to their ships. There was criticism also about the assistance given by the French, who were noticed to hold themselves back. It was supposed they had been given secret orders to let the two sides fight it out and thus weaken one another to the French advantage.

White also quotes a letter from Lord Arlington to the Duke of Lauderdale, with which we might end:

My Lord,   June 1, 72.

Our minds have been very unquiet ever sunce Tuesday last to know what our news would be of the engagement then, and the persecution of it since, the Common relations will best tell your Grace both. All I will say considering the advantage ye enemy took upon us we are well come off and although his Royal Highness had mind enough to have engaged the enemy on Wednesday and had certainly done it if a fog had not miraculously fallen as to prevent it, yet I must confess to your Grace considering all circumstances I am glad we are parted as we are at present. The Dutch have suffered infinitely more than we it is certain; and yet they will not only dissemble it better as to point of reputation, but will be able to appear at sea again much sooner than we can, for they have many ships ready in Holland which they will man with the shattered ones they carry in now, and vapour likewise in that point and have their people of their side more than we shall. His Royal Highness tells the King he will lie in Sole Bay again to refit and take in provisions but his Majesty thinking he may do it with much more despatch and security at the buoy of the Nore hath sent my Lord Clifford to persuade him to it: within twentyfour hours we shall know how he succeeds. The condition the fleet shall be found in will decide the question which by that time will be truly proven with which his Royal Highness hath promised also a true relation of this confused action by that we shall also know what ground there hath been for the severe censures of the behaviour of the French. The King hath this day spoken to the Ambassador to see how he can bring to pass that the 6 or 8 French men of war plying in the channel's mouth for the security of their merchants may be sent hither to strengthen our fleet with which he hath charged himself. I wish your Grace a good progress and success in your voyage and am unfeignedly

> Your Grace's
> most humble and most
> obedient servant
> Arlington.

The Battle was never decided. We claimed a victory, but it was noticed that when the enemy retired we did not pursue.

Tailpiece

The following is taken from *The Eastern Counties Collectanea*, edited by John L'Estrange and published in 1872-3. It had a very short life. The verses were written by Mr Hudson Gurney of Keswick, Norwich, and privately printed.

King in a thousand sixty-six,
Conquest did the Norman fix.
Robert's right to Rufus given,
Saw a thousand eighty-seven.
First Henry first his subjects plundered
In the year eleven hundred.
At the Crown did Stephen arrive
In eleven thirty-five.
In eleven fifty-four,
Henry Plantagenet came o'er.
Reigned eleven eighy-nine,
Richard, dread of Palestine.
John to Pope who did resign,
In eleven ninety-nine.
Henry the Third, in twelve sixteen,
With Lords and Commons first convene.
First Edward resigned twelve seventy-two.
Whose sword did Wales and Scotland rue.
Second Edward, thirteen hundred seven,
Whose road, through tortures, lay to heaven.
In thirteen hundred twenty seven,
To Edward Third the throne was given.
Second Richard, thirteen seventy-seven,
Who thence by Bolingbroke was driven.
Fourth Henry, thirteen ninety-nine,

Begins the proud Lancastrian line.
Fifth Henry comes, fourteen thirteen,
Who conquered France in battle keen.
Sixth Henry, fourteen twenty-two,
Who lost the chance his father threw.
Fourth Edward, fourteen sixty-one,
The regal line of York begun.
In fourteen hundred eighy-three
Fifth Edward crowned and murdered, we
With the third Richard crowned, see.
The white rose sank! the blushing red
But doubtful bloom o'er Tudor shed.
Seventh Henry, fourteen eighty-five,
With Edward's daughter quick to wive.
Whence Henry Eighth, in fifteen nine,
Did claim from the united line.
Sixth Edward, fifteen forty-seven,
First King who ne'er by priests was shriven.
Then Mary, fools of Norfolk, we
Made Queen in fifteen fifty-three,
Who left to Elizabeth her state
In fifteen hundred fifty-eight.
Next Scottish James, "with muckle glee,"
Came south in sixteen hundred three.
First Charles reigned sixteen twenty-five,
Whose neck the Puritans did rive.
In sixteen hundred forty-nine
Did men to Commonwealth incline,
But Cromwell got the mastery
In sixteen hundred fifty-three.
Him dead, was Charles the Second fixt high
Upon the throne in sixteen sixty.
Second James reigned sixteen eighty-five,
Whence him the Whigs did quickly drive,
And took, with Mary, Will her mate,
In sixteen hundred eighty-eight.
In seventeen hundred two or one
The good Queen Anne to reign begun.
First George in seventeen fourteen
From barren Hanover was seen.
Second George in seventeen twenty-seven,
Whose justice did small mercy leaven.
Then George the Third in seventeen sixty
Began to reign and long he sticks t' ye.

Next George the Fourth, in eighteen twenty,
When work was scarce and workmen plenty.
Will, and his Bill, in eighteen thirty,
Some said 't was good, some said it hurt ye.
Victoria last, in thirty-seven,
Whom long may bless and prosper heaven.

INDEX